McGraw Hill   10/15/74   S.O.

CONCILIUM
Religion in the Seventies

CONCILIUM

New Series: Volume 6, Number 10: Theology of Liberation

THE MYSTICAL
AND POLITICAL
DIMENSION OF
THE CHRISTIAN FAITH

Edited by
Claude Geffré and
Gustavo Guttiérez

Herder and Herder

1974
HERDER AND HERDER NEW YORK
815 Second Avenue
New York 10017

ISBN: 0-8164-2580-9

Library of Congress Catalog Card Number: 73-17896
Copyright © 1974 by Herder and Herder Inc. and Stichting Concilium

Printed in the United States

CONTENTS

Editorial
A Prophetic Theology

THERE are now so many books, theses, articles and research projects on the "theology of liberation" that it is just impossible to keep up with them. I would even go so far as to say that it has become something of a myth for European theologians trying to break the bounds of a traditional theology. But there is a great danger of taking up some topics of liberation theology and separating them from the particular socio-ecclesial reality of their origins. The word "liberation" is becoming a magic amulet for theological enterprises which are in fact concerned with contexts outside Latin America. But one thing is certain: it is difficult to "convert" the theology of liberation for the sake of a would-be universal theology if one is not taking part in the struggles of those Christians actually engaged in liberating the South American continent. It is also very difficult to judge it critically from without, inasmuch as the very originality of this form of theological discourse depends on its indissolubility from real practice. Hence, in this special issue of *Concilium*, we have given Latin American theologians an exclusive opportunity to make known their views.

Therefore the articles in this issue should be read as bearing witness to a prophetic theology arising from a particular ecclesial experience, and as a question addressed to the European theology for which *Concilium* is too exclusively a medium. It will be seen that the various articles in this issue, contributed by a team of theologians centring on Gustavo Guttiérez, are not intended to make up an issue on Latin America, but to show from various angles how the historical practice of a specific

7

Church can be an impetus for a new understanding of faith in Jesus Christ. All these theologians are "theologians of liberation". Of course there is no point in examining their articles for a mere reworking of a theme often written on in Europe: that of the relations between "faith and political commitment." Politics is only one of the fields of application for a dynamic faith. In his own way each author tries to show how, on the basis of the specific experience of the Christian communities of Latin America, there is now evident a new connection between the mystical and political dimensions of Christian faith. That was the main intention of this special issue and it appears as an explicit theme in the articles by Segundo Galilea, Gustavo Guttiérez, Ronaldo Muñoz and José Míguez Bonino. Yet, inevitably and significantly, almost all these authors have said something about that special topic of the theology of liberation: the relations between an historical practice of liberation and eschatological salvation. Hence we decided that the general title of this issue should be: "Praxis of Liberation and Christian Faith".

Rather than engage in a critical commentary on the articles in this number, it is important to know how to take the impact of a theology that is not only different and provocative, but sometimes even unjust in regard to certain theologies originating in Europe and North America. But as Europeans we run the risk, with another theological perspective and another practice, of making ill-considered judgments. One of the major contributions of this issue is certainly that of asking us for a more lively awareness of the special and therefore relative nature of our European theology. By way of introduction, all I shall do here is to spell out some of the lessons which most impressed me on reading the subsequent pages.

I. Distancing from Western Theologies

It seems permissible to claim that the episcopal conference at Medellín in 1968, as far as the Latin American Church was concerned, was comparable to Vatican II in its implications for the universal Church. The process which had been maturing for some years among Christians increasingly aware of the challenge to their faith posed by the injustice prevalent on the South

American continent broadened and began to express itself theologically.

The critical discovery of the world of the oppressed as a result of a new scientific consciousness, gradually led to a radical questioning of the existing way of living, understanding and proclaiming the faith. How were people to be Christians in the midst of an exploited and dependent continent, subject to the violence of the established order, under the sign of capitalist domination? How were they to live and conceive the faith within a dynamic movement inspiring and building a more just and fraternal society? The answers to these questions offered by some Christian communities in Latin America start from a position of commitment to the "historical practice of liberation", a practical version of the liberating love of Christ.

In connection with this very special socio-political context, Latin American theologians clearly distance themselves from what has been termed a "neo-integrism" which is developing at present in the USA and some European countries, in order to compensate for the liberal excesses provoked by Vatican II. But, more surprisingly, they criticize even more radically the various "progressive" theologies of the western world—whether "secularization theologies" or "political theology". They share the defect of unconsciously playing the game of western capitalist society. Paradoxically, the secularization theologies which claim to be progressive because they accept the profane nature and autonomy of the modern world, sin by conformism in regard to the neo-liberal societies of the West. Under the pretext that the Church no longer exerts a sociological influence on modern societies, Christianity surrenders its historical efficacy in favour of the transformation of society and the world, and runs the risk of taking refuge in the inwardness of faith. As for German political theology, even though it insists on the historical responsibility of the Church as a court of critical judgment for society as a whole, it remains an abstract and reformist theology which refuses to pronounce on the alternative of socialism or capitalism on the pretext that the eschatological absolute relativizes any practical theological option.

The theology of liberation (see Segundo's article in this issue) wishes to show that the eschatological aspect, far from relativizing the present, connects it to the absolute. It sees in the neutrality of theology towards political choices the influence of the Lutheran thesis of justification by faith without works. In fact Latin American theology deliberately sets out to be a committed theology, both militant and even partisan. It cannot remain neutral in regard to "left" or "right" political positions. Hence it reproaches European theology for its supposed neutrality which, on the pretext of affirming the relativity of the political and the absoluteness of the religious, offers an ideological justification of the established system of the capitalist West. European theologians want to develop a universal theology which will be valid for the whole Church. For Latin American theologians, theology should always start from actual historical practice—for example, the liberation movement on the South American continent. For them, too, a general theology of liberation is quite meaningless.

II. A New Way of Theologizing

The fact that Latin American theology is grounded in an historico-practical context of liberation seriously modifies the traditional conception of theology as understanding of faith. On the one hand, it is a theology which is defined as critical reflection on historical practice in the light of faith. On the other hand, it is a theology which not only addresses itself to interpreting the content of revelation but tries to answer the question, What is to be done?

European theology tries to reformulate the gospel message for today from the basis of the challenge to faith posed by the non-believer. For Latin American theology the challenge does not come primarily from the non-believer but from the non-man: that is, from the one whom the existing social order does not recognize as such: the poor, the exploited, the man who is hardly aware that he is one (see Guttiérez's article). The crucial problem for theology is therefore to know how to announce God as the Father in a non-human world. Hence theology engages in critical reflection on man's historical practice of liberation in confrontation with the word of God lived in faith. In this critical task, theology intends to draw on all the resources of a scientific analysis of the social situation of the Latin American continent, and in particular a Marxist analysis.

Whereas traditional theology started from revelation in order to decide the value of Christian practice, in this case participation in the historical practice of liberation has its own legitimacy and becomes a location of theology by virtue of a reinterpretation of the gospel message, and of a more radical commitment of Christians to revolutionary activity. Distancing itself from an idealist and universal theology claiming to offer an understanding of faith outside an actual context of commitment, this new theology reflects on faith as historical practice: that is, on liberation in regard to this or that situation of oppression as a partial realization of that total and definitive liberation to which Christ bears witness. Therefore it is not only a question of revealing the social and political implications of the Gospel in regard to this or that actual situation, but of making effective participation in the process of liberation the occasion for verifying theological discourse.

Because there can be no hiatus between faith and social practice, it is practice which will judge the truth of a theology. Clearly such a tendency can awaken a suspicion that in making practice the occasion of truth there is a risk of finishing up with a political manipulation of faith or a political reduction of the Gospel. Several contributors to this issue are well aware of that danger. But they all seem to base their answer to it on a theology of the Holy Spirit. It is the Holy Spirit who inspires the activity of the Christian community and who shows Christians the substance of evangelical charity in this or that historical situation. We should juxtapose a theology based on revelation to one based on practice. God also reveals himself through, in and by liberation struggles undertaken by all the poor of the South American continent.

Inasmuch as it is a reflection *in* and *on* practice by those engaged in it, this theology cannot remain content with offering to offer a new theoretical interpretation of Christianity for today. It must address itself to actual problems. It does not answer only the questions, What is to be believed? and What is to be said? It wants to answer the question, What is to be done? This is obviously wholly revolutionary measured against a certain type of theology which considers Christianity mainly as a doctrinal content, hardly ever as action. There is a displacement of the central concern of theology, which is no longer exclusively the *intellectus fidei*, but an understanding of action in the name of Christ: that is, the perception of the forms that love should assume in a specific situation.

That also modifies the conventional conception of the professional theologian. He cannot be merely an exegete and expert on church tradition. He should also be fundamentally concerned to have as rigorous as possible a knowledge of the process of liberation in Latin America. Of course such knowledge is inseparable from an effective part in revolutionary struggles for the liberation of the poor.

A theologian who carries out his theoretical research work independently of actual commitment, as happens in Europe, is inconceivable in Latin America. If this new type of theologian is not defined only as a revelation expert it is clear that this theology is no longer the quasi-exclusive monopoly of clerics who have had many years of training. It is accessible to all the laity participating in Christian communities which are politically committed and which examine their activity critically. But in fact, despite the fact that this possibility is in theory available to the laity, the pioneers of "liberation theology" are almost exclusively priests.

In any case, whatever its limitations and technical inexactitudes we should pay great attention to the rise of this new theology which puts in question the theology of the western world as the dominant ideology of the universal Church. As Dussel says: "... after the major 'Christian theology' (from the fourth to the fifteenth century) and 'modern European theology' (from the sixteenth century to the twentieth) there appears the 'theology of liberation' of the periphery and the oppressed, with whose onset the entire traditional theology begins its paschal movement into the perspective of the poor."

III. A New Theology of Salvation

All the contributors to this issue have examined according to their individual standpoints the process of liberation as a sign of eschatological salvation. Yet Latin American theology is not only a theology *of* liberation or a theology *about* liberation, but a theology which deliberately stands up *for* liberation. We should welcome it as a stimulating and provoking phenomenon in contradistinction to our usual way of posing the question of salvation in Jesus Christ.

Latin American theologians are trying to work out a new image of Jesus Christ and a new conception of salvation by taking as their hermeneutical location the process of liberation occurring at present on the South American continent. That is to say, they reject an abstract theology of liberation which could only take into account the permanent human condition—the state of mankind subject to death, suffering and sin. This type of theology did in fact act as an ideological warning to all those who control political and economic power in Latin America and who are trying to maintain the *status quo*. A "theology of liberation" in general is meaningless. That is why the theologies of liberation are content to be provisional, partial and tentative. They are not easily exportable products which can be used to legitimize Christian activity in other socio-political contexts.

However, these new theologies have a prophetic value in relation to the reinterpretation of Christian salvation which is at present taking place within the Church. Almost everywhere today people are thinking about the connections between "human liberation and salvation in Jesus Christ." And Latin American theology reminds us opportunely that the relation between liberation and salvation is meaningful if it is located historically. In other words, the total and definitive liberation of Christ is always mediated in partial historical liberations.

The necessity for Christian theology in this last quarter of the twentieth century to show forth the bond between the liberation movements in which millions of men are engaged as the coming of the Kingdom of God is not an example of a new ecclesiastical opportunism. In the good sense it is a "sign of the times." The most precious contribution of Latin American theology, rooted as it is in an historical practice of liberation, is to allow us a new understanding of the concept of the "Kingdom of God". As Boff remarks in his article, the Kingdom of God is not only a spiritual reality but a universal revolution of the structures of the old world. That is exactly why it is offered as good news for the poor. The Kingdom of God is not intended to be another world but this old world transformed into a new world, a new order of all the things of this world.

It is right to insist on the anti-messianism of Jesus, on the fact that Jesus avoided the temptation of power during his earthly life. As Boff demonstrates very well in his article, Jesus' temptations stand for a rejection of the "regionalization" of the kingdom, of the reduction of the totality of the kingdom to a particular "province" of this world. But traditional theology argued incorrectly from that to a spiritualization of the Kingdom of God and to a total political neutrality of the Gospel. There was also too much insistence on the absoluteness of the eschatological future of the kingdom, so much so that there was also too much relativization of the historical examples of human liberation which anticipate the total liberation of man as a gift of Christ.

In fact Christ's refusal to be a political messiah is politically significant in itself. That means that Christ does not relieve men of the weight of their historical responsibility for a transformation of the world and society in the direction of God's design. Jesus' historical destiny taken seriously shows us that he did not preach a purely inward kingdom or a salvation which has to do only with the human condition in general, even if it is also true that he did not put forward for us any actual evangelical model which could inspire a Christian politics of liberation today. It is just as true that he came into conflict with the established order of his times and that his death was a political event. In other terms Jesus gave an historical actuality to the Kingdom of God of which he was the witness and of which the mystery of the Resurrection was the definitive epiphany.

Hence the effort of all the poor, whether Christians or not, of Latin America to liberate themselves from economic, political and cultural oppression does not respond merely to a political demand. It is a demand of faith becoming actuality. It is one of the ways of putting the Kingdom of God into practice in history. Of course there can be no identification between the totality of the Kingdom of God and such a process of historical liberation. But there is continuity between the two, for the Kingdom of God is already present "in a mysterious form" in the arena of history.

The Kingdom of God is not wholly available on one occasion but is made incarnate in historical mediations which affect all levels—political, economic, social and religious—of human reality. The coming of the Kingdom is in fact good news for the whole creation. The Latin-American theologians would not hesitate to say that the news of the future kingdom does not make vain the historical struggle of men for their own liberation. Instead it radicalizes it inasmuch as it reveals its transcendent relevance.

IV. A New Kind of Spirituality

To the extent that political liberation is lived as a sign of eschatological liberation, we are becoming aware of a new connection between the mystical and political dimensions of the Christian faith. In all the articles in this issue, despite their variety, it is relatively easy to discern the essentials of a new kind of spirituality which all Christians would do well to consider seriously.

The point of the faith for Latin American Christians is one with the concern to take really seriously the historical implication of Jesus and his salvation—and precisely for the weakest of all, those whose part Christ took. In this way Christians enter into the conflict-ridden and complex world of the poor as a basic choice of their loyalty to the Lord (see the articles by Galilea and Gutiérrez).

This experience of faith on the basis of the world of the poor opens up new horizons for Christian mysticism. The spirituality of liberation may be discerned in the dialectic of loyalty to Jesus and commitment to the poor. In Latin America works of faith are identified with the practice of liberation and are also the actual fruits of life in the Spirit. The contributions in this issue will show how the experience of evangelical conversion as a continual breaking with the egotistic sufficiency of the "old man" in order to enter as a "new man" into the world of the "other", in order to transform it, becomes for Latin American Christians the exercise of liberating love.

To commit oneself to the process of liberation is for a Christian a new way of identifying himself with Christ and constitutes a novel Christian experience, full of promise and possibility, but also of difficulties and disappointments. In fact for many Latin-American Christians liberating commitment corresponds to an authentic spiritual experience in the original, biblical sense of the term: it is living in the Spirit who causes us to acknowledge ourselves in a free and creative way to be sons of the Father and brothers of men.

It is not a question of denying other traditionally valid dimensions of Christian contemplation but rather of rediscovering, by means of integration, the biblical, historical and committed dimensions of contemplation—dimensions which have been forgotten by Christians. This mystical experience presents indivisibly a double dimension of one and the same original event: the meeting with the person of Christ and the experience of the presence of Christ in one's brother, above all in the "least" of one's brothers. The second encounter is the sacrament of the first. Hence it is not a matter of putting contemplation at the service of liberation but of developing its own qualities and, in this case, its biblical dimension of commitment. To speak in those terms, it is to put the socio-political dimension at the heart of Christian mystical experience, as one of its essential constituents. In fact encounter with Christ necessarily occurs through the mediation of the poor brother who exists as an exploited class, as a forgotten race and as a marginalized culture.

*   *   *

The foregoing are a few very fragmentary reflections suggested by the various contributions to the present issue, and which may be of some help to those irritated or puzzled in regard to the present theme. While retaining our critical freedom, we should heed this witness of a prophetic theology which puts in question our conventional ways of thinking and our theological self-sufficiency. Behind this theology in process of formation we must hear the cry of the poor. And what is trying to find its voice and way in Latin America may indeed prefigure what will arise tomorrow in Africa and Asia. The "theologies of liberation" certainly represent an opportunity for the universal Church. And what the theology of the western world might well be tempted to disregard as an "anti-theology" could become the condition of its own renewal.

CLAUDE GEFFRÉ

PART I
ARTICLES

Segundo Galilea

Liberation as an Encounter with Politics and Contemplation

I. The Commitment to Liberation and the Crisis in Spirituality

The term "commitment to liberation" can be misinterpreted because it is ambiguous. Even today in Latin America it can be utilized for ideological or party political ends. At times the impression is given that Christians committed to liberation are to be identified with revolutionary Christians of various political sectors, or even with those who accept to a greater or less degree the Marxist analysis for their diagnosis of injustice in Latin American society. The socio-political options involved in the acceptance of these positions limit the right meaning of commitment or the praxis of liberation. What we have to understand by this latter term—and we take the view of Gustavo Gutiérrez here—is "man's efforts to abolish the present injustice and to construct a different society, freer and more human ... where the oppressed will be agents of their own destiny".[1] This effort not only allows many options to Christians, but is brought about in many ways—through educational work ("education for liberation"), work for cultural or socio-economic advancement and political work. In the present state of society in Latin America, with its strong political emphasis in which changes depend enormously on political decisions, the political dimension is of first importance and in fact tends to be dominant. Hence the political aspect of our commitment to human liberation in Latin America.

[1] G. Gutiérrez, *A Theology of Liberation* (Maryknoll, N.Y. 1973).

The major theologians of Latin American liberation, concerned with faith and not merely with questions related to praxis, coincide in their affirmation that the experience of commitment to liberation has brought Christians into contact with a different cultural world.[2]

This "transculturization" is due to the nature of the activities followed by these committed Christians—politics with its own strategy and rationale, praxis as a criterion of action, and permanent recourse to the human sciences which control the dynamism of society. . . . The Christian is plunged into this world, which is often new to him—in the past it belonged to a few "professional politicians"—and his faith suffers and is called into question.

Generally speaking, the faith of the average Latin American has until now been very clearly defined by his culture. His family, his education, his social environment and the sociological primacy of Catholicism, which gave him a certain image of Christ, ethics and faithful practice all formed part of this "traditional faith". But as soon as the traditional Catholic commits himself to the liberation of the workers or the peasants in tasks of an educational or political nature, he finds himself in a way exiled. The categories of his faith—sin, salvation, charity, prayer, etc.—do not inspire or illuminate sufficiently his commitments. Hence the crisis.

And so, from the pastoral angle, liberation is not only a question of temporal efficacy or of ethics. It is fundamentally also a problem of spirituality. As well as a theology, we need a spirituality of liberation. The Christian's commitment to liberation and within it this primordial socio-political task, is called, like every activity of the believer, to be more than a chance to put into practice the demands of faith and to apply the postulates of charity. It is more than a back-drop to the achievement of salvation. The commitment to liberation in the Christian must be a place of encounter with God, and therefore a source of inspiration to his theological life and his contemplative life. Liberation is the historical and theologico-spiritual place of encounter of the political and contemplative dimensions in the Christian.

[2] Cf. G. Gutiérrez in his article "Liberation, Theology and Proclamation" in this same issue of *Concilium*.

The synthesis between "militant" and "contemplative" is urgent, due to the crisis which we indicated above. This is all the more necessary on account of the misunderstanding which arose in the last thirty years between Christians of different types of spirituality. The last few decades have witnessed two tendencies towards a Christian life style. These can be defined as "religious-contemplative" and "militantly committed". The former looked to strictly "religious" values—prayer and its practice, the liturgy and the sacraments and the transcendent dimensions of Christianity. They were less affected by the temporal or social divisions of the faith.

The latter group emphasize the commitment to historical tasks, social militancy and the praxis of liberation. To varying extents they distrust the inaccurately named "vertical" dimensions of Christianity such as sacramental life, prayer and Christian contemplation in general. One of the important reasons for this dichotomy, which we must now consider more closely, is the ambiguity of the traditional practice of contemplation. Many of its theoretical formulations have not been free of this ambiguity either.

Christian contemplation as "the tranquil dwelling of man in the presence of God"[3] has acquired two different shades of meaning from the early centuries. One came from Platonic mysticism, which in turn was in harmony with oriental mysticism stemming from Buddhism, Hinduism and later Islam. The characteristics of this Platonic contemplation and their indisputable influence, as part of the Greek spirit, on Christian formulations are well known. It has, for instance, a strongly transcendent orientation and neglects bodily, historical, temporal mediations. It tends to make of contemplation an ascent to God in which the temporal sphere is gradually left behind until an exclusive absorption in God is reached. This tendency can easily become a form of escape. This mysticism infected authentic Christian contemplation, not as an isolated fact, but as Greek thought and its dualistic ethos gained influence in the nascent Church.

In questions of spirituality, this was due to a great extent to the writings of Jerome and Cassian, which carried oriental

[3] See K. Rahner and H. Vorgrimler, *Concise Theological Dictionary* (London and New York, 1965), under "Contemplation".

tendencies into Latin spirituality. Cassian himself became the most widely read spiritual author of antiquity and exercised a decisive influence on monachism. For him "Contemplation is a death, an exodus from all earthly things, but at the same time it is also a new life in heaven. The contemplative, having reached the summit of the mountain of contemplation, no longer lives really in the world, but in his true homeland. Resembling the holy angels, he already enjoys their company."[4] The authentic biblical dimension of contemplation, which we call historical or the contemplation of commitment, persisted together with this view. This is the aspect of Christian contemplation which we must recover today in all its fullness, in favour of a renewal of spirituality which will reconcile the contemplative and the political elements in our continent. What is interesting at this moment in Latin America is that this recovery is beginning to be encountered in the experience of many Christians and Christian groups, including those who are committed to various tasks oriented towards liberation.

In these forms of commitment, many believers experience collaboration with the Lord in the redemptive work of building up the Kingdom of God. Many are undergoing a kind of evolution in their dedication to the socio-political field of action. From a tendency to question or even lose their faith they have moved to a position where they now tend to strengthen it, renew prayer and rediscover its meaning. Frequently unprepared for this by their formation, they are discovering a deep affinity between the faith and their options.

These Christians react against an a-historical salvation. They see salvation rather as tied to temporal and political commitments, although they do not reduce it to temporal liberation. They give great importance to the praxis of liberation and discover in prayer the guarantee that evangelical values preside over that praxis. Their commitment itself, at times a very radical one, has led them in many cases to bring their faith to a high degree of Christian mysticism. (In this respect a well-known case is that of Nestor Paz, the Christian *guerrillero* who died four years ago in guerrilla conflicts in Bolivia.)

[4] Quoted by S. Marsili, *Casiano ed Evragio* (Rome, 1936), p. 57.

They see in the practice of their faith the guarantee that their options are governed by love, and that they preserve the ethic sense, and feeling for persons. It is also a guarantee of freedom from pragmatism and from Machiavellian political methods, but it in no way diminishes the intensity of their commitment, or their clarity of vision. Their Christian experience enables them to encounter more creative, human, brotherly ways in liberation, beyond the watchwords of the politicians. They need to experience here and now, the strength of Christian hope in the present-day Latin American historical process, which gives them the certainty that the Kingdom will come. This helps them not to lose heart, to take inspiration from beyond the frequent disillusion of immediate events. Personal, contemplative prayer ensures for them this kind of experience. The Christian committed to liberation becomes a contemplative to the extent that he grasps what God wishes for his fellow man and makes that the decisive motive for his commitment. He also becomes capable of preserving the universality of love, without renouncing his preference for the oppressed.[5]

II. Contemplation and Commitment

These experiences are not pure intuitions without Christian values. They go to meet the biblical, historical, committed dimension of contemplation, much neglected among us.

Renewal through integration is sought here, without any rejection of other traditionally valid dimensions of Christian contemplation, in particular its dimension of gratuitous adoration and the value of loving and contemplating God for himself. The dimension that concerns us now relates to the fact that contemplation is essentially linked to the vigour of faith, and to the capacity of faith to bathe life and history in a new light. Contemplation means having an experience of God, real though obscure, in all dimensions of human life. It is the capacity to encounter Christ, and the experience of encountering him, through a vigorous, incarnate faith (1 John 1. 1) "... which we have heard, which we have seen with our eyes, which we have

[5] See the report of S. Galilea, "Spiritual Awakening and the Movements of Liberation in Latin America", in *Concilium*, Nov. 1973 (American edn., Vol. 89).

looked upon and touched with our hands, concerning the word of life. . .". John's witness is always found in the contemplative in the experience of his faith.

This experimental encounter with God, which is revealed to us in Christ, assumes the two contemplative encounters conveyed by the Gospel. The first is that of the person of Jesus. In the New Testament, this encounter is the root of every conversion to the faith and the contemplative life. Christ's revelation to the men of his time (Zacchaeus, the Samaritan woman, Peter, the disciples of Emmaus, etc.) created in them a contemplative encounter and experience. Each one of them is a type of the Christian, and to be a Christian and have met Jesus is one and the same thing in the New Testament. The same contemplative encounter happened to the Apostles and was expressed in the experience of I John I. I. It appears as identified with the apostolic vocation in the Transfiguration (Matthew 17. 1–8). This episode corresponds to the discovery of a new dimension of Christianity, a contemplative dimension which goes beyond action. ("It is well that we are here: if you wish, I will make three booths here.") The encounter with the person of Jesus acquires for the apostles a value in itself; it is privileged and surpasses at that moment the experience of action. Paul also had the same type of encounter (2 Cor. 12; Phil. 3, 7 ff.) and it is found in the experience of all the saints.

The second encounter is inseparable from and complementary to that of the person of Christ. It is the contemplative experience of the presence of Christ in one's brother, particularly one's "little brother". It is typified in the famous pericope of Matthew 25. 31: "I was hungry, and you gave me food . . . as you did to one of the least of these my brethren, you did it to me." Here the encounter with the needy and suffering brother (the "least") and the consequent service to him is an experience of Christ— it is contemplative in this sense of being a personal encounter with the Lord. Both encounters are inseparable. The first emphasizes that Christianity transcends any temporal reality, the second that it is incarnate and inseparable from the love for one's brother. The first recalls the first commandment of the love of God above all things, and the absolute of the person of Jesus. The second recalls the commandment similar to the first, the love of one's neighbour as oneself, and the presence of Christ in this love. The first encounter derives from contemplative prayer and the various ways of relating to God, the second from temporal commitment as a Christian experience. The second encounter "incarnates" the first, and gives an historical dimension to the encounter with God and to our life of prayer.

The experience of Jesus in service to our brother gives the Christian consciousness its social dimension and frees it of any tendency to be purely individual, private or platonic. It gives brotherly love a social, collective dimension to the extent that the "least" are not only individual persons in Latin America, but human groups—marginal subcultures, social classes or sectors. There is in them a collective presence of Jesus, the experience of which constitutes a true contemplative act.

Contemplation conceived in this way gives a socio-political content to faith and itself acquires an historico-social dimension, without being reduced to this alone. Christ encountered and contemplated in prayer is prolonged in the encounter with our brother and, if we are capable of experiencing Christ in our service of the "least", it is because we have already encountered him in contemplative prayer. Contemplation is not only the discovery of the presence of Jesus in the brother ("you did it to me") but also a call to action in his favour, to the liberating commitment ("as you did it..."). The contemplation of Christ in the suffering, oppressed brother is a call to commitment. It is the historical content of Christian contemplation in the Latin American Church.

The service-encounter with the poor is contemplative in believers, and makes of them "contemplatives in action", in the purest Christian tradition. This is not an automatic experience —it occurs as the Christian becomes conscious of Christ encountered in prayer, as a back-drop to action. The Other experienced in contemplative prayer is also experienced in the encounter with the others.

This encounter with Christ in others is not improvised. It assumes that he has been contemplated in prayer and this experience is reactivated in the service of others and so acquires a social, historical content and purifies our orientation towards others.[6]

[6] K. Rahner and H. Vohrgrimler, *op. cit.*

Dedication to our brother and his liberation, considered as a contemplative experience, implies an accompanying and intuitively illuminating presence of that same Christ encountered in prayer. This consciousness of Christ is the point where prayer and commitment unite, and it prevents the latter from becoming hollow and empty, by including them both in the same contemplative experience. Christian mysticism is a mysticism of commitment.

III. The Mystical and Political Dimension of Contemplation

These reflections call for a reformulation or perfection of the idea of contemplation, while preserving its traditional values and especially its gratuitous quality and its transcendence of any element of "utilitarianism" which may place it at the service of profane or apostolic tasks. Contemplative prayer is not to be placed at the service of liberation. The aim is rather to open up all its potentialities, in this case above all its dimension of commitment.

The essence of true Christian prayer has always consisted in going out of oneself to encounter the Other who is God. Far from being a kind of egoistic approach, an escape from realities and responsibilities, true prayer is the supreme act of abnegation and forgetfulness of self in order to encounter Christ and his demands in others. In this sense prayer is related to the classical themes of the cross and death. According to Paul's teaching in Romans, we were crucified with Christ and having died with him we are now alive for God in him. This implies the crucifixion of egoism and the purification of the self as a condition of contemplation. This crucifixion of egoism in forgetfulness of self in the dialectic prayer-commitment will be brought to fulfilment both in the mystical dimension of communication with Jesus in the luminous night of faith, and also in the sacrifice which is assumed by commitment to the liberation of others. The "death" of mysticism and the "death" of the militant are the two dimensions of the call to accept the cross, as the condition of being a disciple (Mt. 16. 24).

Solitude, aridity and the dark night accompany the exercise of contemplation and are a means to purge egoism and go out of oneself to encounter the Other. These are also found in the commitment of the Christian to the service of the other. To discover him as the other to whom I must dedicate myself, and not as an extension of myself and my own interests, it is necessary to go out of myself, to die, to crucify egoism through a dark night of contradictions and a prolonged apprenticeship to brotherly love. We purify ourselves for God, to the extent that we purify ourselves for our brother and vice versa.

This capacity to live for one's brother, especially if he is poor and little, is the decisive source of the temporal commitment of the Christian and of the socio-political dimension of his faith and charity. It is the basis of the public and social dimension of contemplation, until now unduly "privatized" and wrapped in mystery. It is there, not in the dialectic of the class struggle, that believers will find the strength for their militancy and their work for liberation.

Close to the theme of purification, the cross and death, is found that of the desert, an equally traditional theme in Christian spirituality. Here also we must rediscover its double dimension, mystical and political. The desert in Christian tradition is first and foremost a spiritual attitude. However, many of the great contemplatives, including Jesus himself (Mt. 4. 1), Paul (Gal. 1. 17), many prophets (Ezechiel, Jeremiah, Moses and Elias, to whom we will return later), the early monks, many contemplative orders and Charles de Foucauld in modern times, went to the geographical desert at many periods of their lives, so as to feel this attitude with the help of an external setting. The geographical desert is the symbol of an attitude of self-emptying and of taking up one's place in truth and without illusions before God. It is an attitude of radical poverty which leads one to place all one's hope in the gift of Christ, of silence in order to listen to the word of the Other.

The desert is an attitude of human powerlessness in the presence of salvation. It is a disposition to receive this salvation gratuitously in the painful experience of one's own limitations and with the obscure conviction that God seeks us out and that Christianity, rather than man's love of God, is the love of Jesus seeking out man first.

The desert has been conceived almost exclusively in relation to the mystical life of prayer and in the context of the first encounter of the New Testament to which we referred previously, which is the contemplative relationship with the person of Jesus. We believe that to rediscover the authentic concept of Christian contemplation, in a form bearing significance for those believers who are committed to liberating action, the experience of the desert would also have to be extended to the second encounter, the encounter of Christ with the least of his brethren.

The attitude of the desert, a contemplative attitude, is united to this commitment. The desert forged the great prophets, and present-day Christian prophecy in Latin America likewise needs the contemplative attitude of the desert. The attitude of going out of oneself, of re-encountering the Absolute and the true reality of things appropriate to the desert allows the Christian to leave the system, to regard it as an unjust and false society, to condemn it and to become free of it. If the Christian does not withdraw to the desert in order to make an interior withdrawal from the system, he will not become free or a prophet of liberation for others. If he has not managed to create silence within himself in order to shut out the words of oppression and listen to the word of "the truth which makes us free", he will not be able to transform his milieu prophetically or politically. The desert as a political experience liberates him from egoism and from the "system", and is a source of freedom and of an ability to liberate.

Authentic Christian contemplation, passing through the desert, transforms contemplatives into prophets and heroes of commitment and militants into mystics. Christianity achieves the synthesis of the politician and the mystic, the militant and the contemplative, and abolishes the false antithesis between the religious-contemplative and the militantly committed. Authentic contemplation, through the encounter with the absolute of God, leads to the absolute of one's neighbour. It is the meeting-place for this difficult symbiosis which is so necessary and creative for Latin American Christians committed to the liberation of the poor.

IV. Contemplation and Prophecy in the Biblical Message

Current Christian witness to the synthesis of commitment and contemplation and the restoration of its authentic content are rooted in the best tradition of Christianity and the Bible. The prophets follow this line and guide the people, criticize the system, act as spokesmen of a message of liberty. They do this not from the vantage-point of power politics, but from the people themselves and service of the people and also from the contemplation of the Word of God which impels them to act. This is the mystical political attitude of the Christian, beginning from the people and the Word and not from the egoism of power. The prophetic figure of Elijah could be an inspiration to these Christians of today. Scripture shows this prophet on fire with God's zeal (1 Kings 19. 10) and this zeal and solicitude were revealed to him in the desert, where he had to flee (17. 2 ff; 19. 4–8). From the desert, God led him to the contemplation of his face, manifesting himself in the same place where Moses saw the Lord (9. 9–14). This manifestation is not spectacular but is "the sound of a gentle breeze" (19. 12) like a sign of the intimacy of God with the contemplatives and prophets. Like Moses, Elijah was converted by his encounter with God into a source of justice for his people (19. 15–18).

Transformed by this encounter with his Lord, Elijah was able to confront the potentates and oppressors of his time, who were intoxicated by military victories and material splendours and who wallowed in a climate of pride and national exultation (16. 23–4). In the temple of Baal hundreds of false prophets sustained and propagated the worship of idols. Elijah accepted the commitment which God offered him to confront this power system and liberate the people from idolatrous oppression. The confrontation reached its crisis on Mount Carmel (18. 25 ff.) where God was by Elijah's side, confounding the enemy with his gratuitous intervention.

Every time God's rights were at stake, Elijah once again became prophetically committed (2 Kings 1). He did so not only respecting the cult of idols and questions of religion, but also respecting justice and the faith of the weak. This was the case in his prophetic denunciation of Ahab, the King of Samaria, the murderer and usurper of the possessions of the defenceless Naboth (1 Kings 21). The king eventually repented and was converted.

In the New Testament, the symbol of Elijah as a contemplative and committed prophet is offered to all Christians. John the Baptist, the greatest of the prophets, is presented in this line (Mt. 11. 14), and James puts him forward as a model of faith and prayer, since he was "a human being like ourselves" (James 5. 17). In Matthew 17. 1 ff., his dialogue with the transfigured Jesus, as previously with Yahweh in the whisper of the breeze, has stood in the Christian tradition as the symbol of the contemplative prophet.[7]

The figure of Moses must also be seen in this line as typical of the mystical politician, who had a profound experience of God in the desert, and without ceasing to be guided by this experience, led a people towards their liberation.

In this enterprise, the contemplative quality of Moses led him to an encounter with the absolute of the Other in the solitude of the burning bush and with the absolute of the others in whom his experienced faith caused him to discover a people indwelt by Yahweh, to which he was to communicate the freedom of the children of God. This contemplative quality also enabled this mystic to avoid "mythifying" a people who were frequently mediocre; and to accept therefore the lonely task of prophetic guidance. "Why does Yahweh bring us to this land? Should we not do better to go back to Egypt? Let us appoint a leader and go back. Why did you lead us out of Egypt only to bring us to this wretched place" (Num. 14 and 20).

In this prophetic solitude, Moses nevertheless remained firm in hope, as if he had seen the invisible since because of his contemplative faith "he considered that the insults offered to Christ were more precious than all the treasures of Egypt" (Heb. 11. 26–27).

This hope which is so characteristic of political prophecy led Moses to the limit of sacrifice in his mission and in the end he himself did not enter the promised land to which he had led the people. He sacrificed "power" to the "liberating service of the people", faithful to his mission.

[7] Cf. X. Leon-Dufour, *Dictionary of Biblical Theology* (New York, 1968).

The Latin American theology of liberation has restored the Exodus to its political symbolism and has seen in Moses an authentic politician, guiding the people towards a better society.[8]

If the Christian politician in Latin America has to have a spirituality adequate to his mission and commitments, he has an inspiring model in Moses. In his political activity this prophet (and the Christian politician at the present moment in the continent ought to be a prophet) kept the wider significance of his mission alive. He knew that the political liberation from Egypt fitted into a much wider and more integral divine plan for the eschatological salvation of the people. He knew that his activity would remain always incomplete, at times frustrated, at times rejected, because the unique and definitive liberator of the people was not himself, but God, whose Kingdom would have no end. So he dedicated himself up to the end, because the hope that animated him came not from himself, but was renewed daily in him, in his encounter with his Lord. And is hope not the great inspiring virtue of the politician?

In a different dimension, the message delivered to us by the Messianism of Jesus is also profoundly illuminating. In him, contemplation reverts to a commitment not directly temporal, but prophetic and pastoral, with socio-political consequences, more fitted for the ministry of evangelization than for temporal political action.

The commitment of the contemplative to the poor and the little can be specified along two directions. The first is the straight political option. In this, the Christian canalizes his charity—the service of Christ in the other—through the mediation of projects. For this, he needs to share in power. That is the basis of his party political option, in which charity, for him, finds its most effective channel of liberation. Here his contemplative commitment becomes strategy and party politics.

The second direction of the commitment to the "least" is that of the prophetic pastoral option. In it charity, the source of con-

[8] G. Gutíerrez, op. cit. E. Pironio, "Teología de la liberación in Criterio 1606 (Buenos Aires 1970), p. 786; H. Assmann, Opresión-liberación, desafío a los cristianos (Montevideo, 1971), p. 71; R. Alves, "El pueblo de Dios y la liberación del hombre" in Fichas de ISAL, 3 (Montevideo 1970), pp. 9 ff.) and many others. On this point the consensus of authors is remarkable.

templation, is channelled into the effective proclamation of the message of Christ about the liberation of the poor and the "least". The message becomes a critical consciousness, and is capable of inspiring the deepest and most decisive liberating transformations. In this sense it has social and political consequences. This option is more charismatic and therefore it is less widespread.

Committed charity needs both of these forms of expression, and one does not necessarily exclude the other. Human love also finds its expression in two ways—in marriage and in the less widespread and more charismatic modality of celibacy. Both forms of living are potent, like the two kinds of commitment which we have noted, and both are effective and legitimately Christian. The second kind, more appropriate to the pastoral ministry and the hierarchy—although it does not absolutely exclude other forms of commitment—is the kind of militancy which Christ himself and the apostles adopted. With it, they renounced power and politics, but in return they brought about the conditions of consciousness necessary for progressive liberation from all forms of oppression.

When Christ and the apostles revealed the presence of God in every human being, and with it the dignity and absolute destiny of man, they not merely expressed their own contemplative vision of man, but endowed this prophetic announcement with a socio-political content, making it incompatible with the prevailing social system and with pagan attitudes towards human beings.

By giving the poor and little a privileged place and identifying himself specially with them, Christ called the poor to the Kingdom of God and mobilized them. This is not only a mystic act—"to intuite" the presence of Jesus in the dispossessed, so discovering their dignity—but it leads to social commitment and to political consequences, since this incorporation of the poor in the Kingdom of God passes through history and implies a progressive liberation of the same poor and little from concrete social systems.

Jesus proclaimed the beatitudes. It is impossible to announce and live this message without living in hope, in other words, without being a contemplative. But the beatitudes themselves from the ethical attitude of the contemplatives. This radical modality of living and gospel is a prophecy which invariably questions individuals and societies.

Thus, the biblical message from Moses to Jesus shows us the two aspects of the liberating commitment of faith. In Moses, liberation takes on a temporal, political expression, and in Christ it shows forth the full sense of liberation.

This full meaning is established in Jesus. Liberation is seen as decisive, eschatological, saving and transforming from within man and society. It implies a socio-political transformation, just as the liberation of Moses implied the conversion of the heart and the eschatological vocation of Israel.

We have here incarnate the mystic-prophetic dimension and the political dimension of faith and contemplation. Latin American Christians live out these dimensions in varying degrees in their daily lives, but they always complement each other in accordance with the individual's function or vocation. The mystic and the politician are united in one same call to contemplation, since the source of their Christian vision is the same—the experience of Jesus encountered in prayer and in our brothers, particularly the "least" (Mt. 25. 41).

Translated by J. P. Donnelly

Enrique Dussel

Domination—Liberation:
A New Approach

THIS article is divided into two parts. The first part consists of a detailed analysis of some of the themes currently prevailing in Latin American theology. This is followed, in Part II, by a methodological analysis to show the relevance of this theology not only for our Latin America, but for all "peripheral" cultures —in fact for theology throughout the world, beyond the bounds, that is, of strictly European theology.

I. DOMINATION—LIBERATION

In this first section we shall examine in detail the trends taken by Latin American theology, which always starts, not from a theological position, but from the state of affairs as they actually exist. We start, therefore, not with what theologians have said about the situation, but with the situation itself. As we can indicate only some of the themes possible, we shall consider the three which tradition suggests should be the most important. In Semitic thought Hammurabi declared quite clearly in his *Code*: "I have defended them with wisdom, so that the strong shall not oppress the weak, and that justice be done to the orphan and widow." These political, sexual and educational levels are also indicated in Isa. 1. 17: "Correct oppression; defend the fatherless; plead for the widow." The same three levels are also indicated by Jesus: "Truly I say to you, there is no man who has left house, or wife or parents or children ..." (Lk. 18. 29). In the sixteenth century, Bartolomé de las Casas accused European

Christians of injustice because "the men—for in battles normally only children and women are left alive—are oppressed with the hardest, most horrible and harshest servitude."[1] The brother-to-brother aspect (male, oppressed, weak) is the political level; the man-woman aspect (home, wife, widow) is the sexual level; the father-son aspect (orphan, child) is the educational level. Let us see how, on these three levels, an argument can be constructed from the situation as it acutally exists.

1. *The Political Starting-Point*

The present world situation reveals in its structure an imbalance that is already five centuries old. Byzantine Christianity was destroyed in 1453 and, thanks to the experiences of Portugal in North Africa and the failure of its eastward expansion (the conquest movement of the crusades in the Middle Ages which tried to reach the Orient by way of the Arab world), Latin Christianity began to expand in the North Atlantic, which has remained, up to the present day, the centre of world history, politically speaking. First Spain, then Holland and England, followed by France and other European countries, worked out the framework of a truly world-wide oikumene, for until the fifteenth century the Latin, Byzantine Arab, Indian, Chinese, Aztec or Inca oikumenes were purely regional. The new oikumene had its centre in Europe and, since the end of the nineteenth and beginning of the present century, the United States, Russia, and more recently Japan. It also had a huge periphery —Latin America, the Arab world, Black Africa, South East Asia, India and China.

European man first said, through Spain and Portugal, with Pizarro and Cortés: "I conquer"—and he said it to the Indian. With Hobbes he stated more clearly still: "Homo homini lupus." With Nietzsche he called himself "the will to power". Thus the political and economic structure of the world was unified into

[1] *Brevísima relación de la destrucción de las Indias* (Buenos Aires, 1966), p. 36. For an historical insight into the argument of this present article, see my *Historia de la Iglesia en América Latina. Coloniaje y liberación (1492–1972)* (Barcelona, 1972); for the theological matter see *Caminos de liberación latino-americana,* two volumes (Buenos Aires, 1972–73); for the philosophical background, *Para una ética de la liberación latino-americana,* three volumes (Buenos Aires, 1973–74).

one all-powerful international market. Here is an example to illustrate the profound moral injustice of this dehumanizing structure.

EXPORTS OF PRECIOUS METALS FROM THE PRIVATE SECTOR TO EUROPE, WITH CORRESPONDING IMPORTS OF MERCHANDISE INTO LATIN AMERICA (In maravedis, the currency of the period).

Period	Exports from the private sector	Imported goods	Balance in Spain's favour
1561–1570	8,785 million	1,565 million	7,220 million
1581–1590	16,926 ,,	3,915 ,,	13,011 ,,
1621–1630	19,104 ,,	5,300 ,,	13,804 ,,

(Source: Works of Alvaro Jara, Pierre Chaunu, Osvaldo Sunkel.)

This dependence and colonial injustice was to last without interruption from the sixteenth to the twentieth century. Raul Prebisch tells us in 1964 that, between 1950 and 1961 in Latin America, "net remissions of foreign capital of all types reached the figure of 9,600 million dollars, while Latin American exports overseas amounted to 13,400 million dollars."[2] So far as the political situation is concerned (brother-to-brother) domination is now exercised by the centre over the periphery. This pattern is repeated when the capital city exploits the interior or the provinces,[3] or where an upper-class minority dominates the

[2] *Nueva política comercial para el desarrollo* (Mexico, 1966), p. 30. If to this is added the deterioration in price-ratios between raw materials and manufactured products, the so-called under-developed countries have been simply exploited, expropriated and robbed. From this bulletin of CEPAL (UNESCO) came the so-called social economy of dependence based on the works of Celso Furtado, Jaguaribe, Cardoso, Faletto, Theotonio dos Santos, Gunter Frank or Hinkelammert in Latin America or of Samir Amin in Africa, with the European position given by Arghiri Emmanuel or Charles Bettelheim. See also a bibliography on the subject in *Desarrollo y revolución, Iglesia y liberación (Bibliografía)* produced by CEDIAL, Bogotá, Parts 1 & 2 (1971–3).

[3] In the presidential elections in Argentina on 23 Sept. 1973, the Federal Capital (Buenos Aires) awarded the working/peasant class candidate 42% of the votes, while the poorest provinces in the north-east awarded more

working classes, and where bureaucracy directs the fortunes of the masses.

2. *The Sexual Starting-Point*

Interpersonal relations show that in the relationship of man to woman, injustice has existed for thousands of years—an injustice which reached its highest level in modern Europe. If it is true, as Freud so brilliantly revealed, that, in our male-dominated society, "the *libido* is generally masculine in nature",[4] it was not so clearly seen that the colonizer was usually male and his victim in our case was the Indian woman. Bishop Juan Ramírez of Guatemala, wrote on March 10th, 1603: "The worst forms of force and violence, unheard of in other nations and kingdoms, are perpetrated upon the Indian women. The wives of Indian men are raped forcibly by order of the authorities and they are obliged to work in the homes of planters, on farms and in labour camps where they live in sin with the master of the house, with mestizos, mulattos, blacks, or with other cruel men".[5] The colonial male who lies illegally with the Indian woman is the father of the mestizo, and the Indian woman is the mother. The male conquistador—first the planters and colonial bureaucracy, later the native-born creole minority and finally the bourgeoisie of the dependent territories—sexually oppressed and alienated the Indian, the mestizo or the poor woman. The male from the national higher-class minority seized the local girl from the hands of the poor working man living on the outskirts of the big cities—a theme sung in the Tango "Margot" 1918, by Celedonio Flores—while demanding of his own high-born wife both purity and chastity. This particular piece of hypocrisy was pointed out by W. Reich and it can be observed extensively in the Third World.

---

than 75% (Jujuy, Salta, Tucumán, Santiago del Estero, Catamarca, La Rioja). The big Latin American capitals provide evidence of internal dependence.

[4] *Three Contributions to the Theory of Sex*, III, 4. Freud's error consists in confusing "the reality of masculine domination in our society with the "reality of sexuality" as such. See my "Para una erótica latinoamericana" (chapter VII in *Para una ética de la liberación latinoamericana*, III, pp. 42–7).

[5] *Archivo General de Indias* (Seville), Audiencia de Guatemala 156.

The everyday "I conquer", the ontological *ego cogito*, comes from the oppressor male, who, as we see by psychoanalysis of Descartes, denies his mother, his lover and his daughter. To borrow an expression from Maryse Choisy and Lacan, we might say that these days "phallocracy goes hand-in-hand with pluto-cracy".

3. *The Educational Starting-Point*

Political and sexual domination is completed through *educa-tion*: the child is conditioned within the family, and youth in society is moulded through the media. Since Aristotle[6] educators have maintained that "parents love their children because they regard them as they regard themselves (*heatous*), for they are in some sense one's self (*tauto*), yet divided into separate indivi-duals" (*Et. Nic.* VIII, 12, 1161 b 27–34). Cultural conquest of other peoples is equally an expansion of the self. The conquis-tador or the propagandist achieves his aim by force of arms or by violently imposing on the other (the Indian, African, Asian, the community, the worker, the oppressed) so-called civilization, or his religion, or by exalting his own cultural system (the ideo-logical closed system). Educational domination is dialectical (from the Greek *dia* = through)—a movement whereby the cultural boundaries of the father, the imperialist or the obligarchy extend so as to embrace the other (the son) within its self. The process of conquest and cultural assimilation in America, Africa and Asia and the education of the son into the self (as Socrates proposed in his mayeutica as a means of "being delivered of one's ideas") is a kind of inverted Passover, an ideological dialectic whereby the new being (the other, the young person) is eclipsed and domination made complete. Further, it is projected into the personal and social ego, so that the son or the oppressed culture even begins to sing the praises of his oppressor: "two different civilizations can be seen side by side—the one belonging to the country itself and the other to European civilization."[7] Sarmiento spurns the culture of the periphery, the dependent nation, the

---

[6] See my *Para una ética de la liberación, op. cit.,* pp. 137 ff.
[7] Domingo F. Sarmiento, *Facundo* (English trans.)

gaucho and the poor; instead he exalts the culture of the "centre", which is a minority culture, élitist and oppressive.

4. *Face-to-Face Encounter—the Closed System and the Outside*

Starting-point of our argument was the "actual situation" or (reality) considered at three levels. But reality can have two different basic meanings. Anything within the world is real as having existence in the world[8] and in this sense the Indian was a real being assigned to a master and the Black was a real being, who was enslaved. On the other hand, something can also be real from a universal point of view[9] as constituted by its essential physical structure.[10] The political, sexual and educational points we have made are events taking place within various situations, with men playing different roles, whether as dependent under-developed countries, as woman or as child. These situations are, however, distortions or denials of that very basic human (one might even say, sacred) quality—face-to-face encounter. The real situation of men *within* circumstances of oppression is a denial of the real nature of man as "another being",—which is the metaphysical meaning of reality.

Encounter face-to-face (Hebrew *pnîm'el pnim* of Ex. 33. 11), person-to-person encounter (Greek *prosopon pros prosopon*, 1 Cor. 13. 12), is a linguistic reduplication, common in Hebrew, used to convey the greatest nearness of comparison—the very closest in this case: closeness, the immediacy of contact between two mysteries each equally aware of meeting another. In sexual activity this encounter is mouth-to-mouth—i.e. the kiss: "Oh that you would kiss me with the kisses of your mouth!" (Song

[8] This is the meaning of reality for Heidegger, *Being and Time* (New York, 1962).
[9] Expression used by the older Schelling (*Einleitung in die Philosophie der Mythologie*, XXIV); *Werke*, V (Munich, 1959), p. 748; *transmundan*, though not with the same meaning. Beyond being and beyond the world, is the Lord of being (*ibid.*).
[10] Xavier Zubiri, *Sobre la escencia* (Madid, 1963), p. 395: "Reality is the object as something in its own right. The object is actualized in the mind and presents itself to us intellectually as existing in its own right before (*prius*) we actually see it." In the same sense the other for Levinas is the reality beyond the closed system and beyond being (cf. *Totalité et Infini*, The Hague, 1961). See also my *La Dialectica hegeliana* (Mendoza, 1972), pp. 141 ff.

of Songs 1. 1). This is a fundamental truth, a *veritas prima*—to see the face of someone without oneself losing the quality of someone; to see the face of the other, and yet to remain oneself; to encounter the mystery which opens out, incomprehensible and sacred beyond the eyes that I actually see and which actually see me in the closeness of encounter.

There was a day when the conquistador stood face-to-face with the Indian, the African and the Asian. The boss stood face-to-face with the unemployed who came to seek work. The man was face-to-face with the helpless woman begging for mercy. The father stood before his new-born son, face-to-face, as a man talking to his intimate friend. With its closed system (the ontological), Europe opened itself as the male and the father was open to the otherness (the metaphysical if *physics* is "being" in the sense of the world's horizons) of the peripheral cultures, to the woman and child, or, we might say, to the "stranger, the widow and the orphan", as the prophets had it.

The other is primary (the parents who beget the son, the society which admits us into its traditions or the Creator who gives us real being). Man, rather than relate to nature (the economic level), chooses to expose himself to another man. We are born in the womb of a someone (our mother); in our first waking moments we eat that someone (we suckle at the breasts of our mother). We ardently want to remain face-to-face ever afterwards. After the closeness of face-to-face relationship the separation necessitated by economic dealings is a painful alternative.

5. *The Oppressor Praxis—Sin and the Poor*

Biblical symbolism shows us through the prophetic tradition an argument or line of thought which we shall here set out briefly. In the first place "Cain rose up against his brother Abel, and killed him" (Gen. 4. 8), and Jesus adds the comment "innocent Abel" (Mt. 23. 25). To say "no" to my neighbour is the only possible sin, it is the "sin of the world" or the fundamental sin. The same "no" to my neighbour is said by the priest and the levite in the parable of the Samaritan (Lk. 10. 31–2). Augustine, in his political interpretation of original sin, says clearly that "Cain founded a city, while Abel the wanderer did not".[11] Historically and actually sin since the fifteenth century has taken the form of a "no" on the part of the North Atlantic centre to the Indian, the African, the Asian and to the worker, the peasant and the outcast. It has been a "no" to the woman in patriarchal families, and a "no" to the child in the oppressor's educational system.

"No" to my neighbour (anthropologically speaking) or fratricide leads to maximizing the reign of the "flesh" (*basar* in Hebrew; *sarx* in Greek). The device of *temptation* (and not of Prometheus bound to the *ananke*) is the one proposed by the closed system in the words, "You shall be as gods" (Gen. 3. 5). Sin, beginning as "no" to my neighbour, takes the form of self-deification, the exalting of self as an object of worship, and leads to idolatry—"no" to the Creator. To be able to say with Nietzsche "God is dead" it was necessary first of all to kill his manifestation of himself to the Indian, the African and the Asian.

Idolatrous exaltation of the *flesh*, in this case as seen in the modern structure of European Christianity, produces within the closed system a separation between the one who dominates "the world" (a new term for "*flesh*", but now completely deified) and the oppressed. On the one side stand "the rulers" (*archontes*) of the nations (who) lord it over them (*katakyrieousin*) and the great men (who) exercise authority" (Mt. 20. 25). These are the "angels" (sent by) the "Prince of this world" and the Pilates who "ask for water and wash their hands" (Mt. 27. 24). The present world order (economic, cultural, sexual and aesthetic) is the prevailing rule of sin, inasmuch as it oppresses the poor. The "rulers" have their group projection which they objectivize as the projection of the whole system and which expands as an imperialist projection by means of conquest in Latin America, Africa and Asia. The "self" remains the "self". The "praxis of domination" of those who ursurp the position of God and exalt themselves is sin in a very real and strict sense. This is the praxis of "no" to my neighbour, spoken to the op-

[11] *Civ. Dei,* XV, 1. *Civ. Dei* expounds the two basic biblical categories: the "closed-shop" founded on self-seeking love (*libido*), and openness which lies open to the future in loving concern for others (*caritas*). See *Para una ética de la liberación latinoamericana,* Chap. IV, §§ 20–23, and Chap. V, §§ 26–8, volume II, pp. 13–88.

pressed brother, to woman as a sexual object, to the child as the unthinking reproducer of traditional ways of life.

The oppressed one is Job. He suffers because sin (the praxis of the great one acting as *oppressor*) alienates him, but he is not aware of having committed any sin at all. The wise men in his situation, speaking for the system (Bildad and Sophar), try to convince the oppressed one in the name of Satan, that he is a sinner. By so doing they maintain the innocence of the real sinner— of the oppressors.

The oppressed one humanly speaking is not the poor (the oppressed as an other). The "poor" in the words "Blessed are the poor" (*ptochoi*) (Lk. 6. 20), or better still in the words "The poor you shall have with you always" (Mt. 26. 11) is the other in that he does not share the supreme value of the socio-political system. The "poor" are just as much a category—they are the oppressed nation, class, person or woman in that these are outside the structure of the oppressor. In this sense the "poor" (in the biblical sense) are not the same as the alienated oppressed living *within* the system, but they do share many of the characteristics of the poor socially and economically speaking.

6. The Praxis of Liberation—Redemption and the Prophet

To make the contrast with the "praxis of sin" set out in the previous section, we can now look at the praxis of liberation, of anti-sin or the direct opposite of the negation of the other.[12] The Bible speaks, in the story of Moses (Ex. 3 ff.) or in the parable of the Samaritan, of a direct "yes" to my neighbour when he is still oppressed within the system. The prophetic light of faith permits us to see through the outward surface of the oppressed and to see the other within. Behind the slave of Egypt lies man, liberated. Behind the beaten, robbed traveller lying at the roadside

---

[12] In Hegel this is the negation of distinction and the object, which for its part has been the negation of Being in itself or Totality taken as the originating and divine Identity. On the other hand, in our case it is a matter of denying the alienation of the other (reduced to the level of an object), that is to say, to affirm (say "yes" to) the other who is distinct. (See my *Para una ética de la liberación*, chap. III, § 16, vol. I, pp. 118 ff.; chap. IV, § 23, and chap. V, §§ 29-31, vol. II, pp. 42-127); thus this is a negation of what Hegel affirmed coming from an Outside unknown to him.

is the otherness of the human *persona*. This is not a turning aside (*aversio*) from the other, but a turning towards (*conversio*) the other as a fellow citizen of the City of God. As we see in the case of Bartolomé de las Casas, that ardent anti-conquistador and modern European, the righteous man discovers the other as he really is: "God made these people (the Indians) the simplest of men, without guile or cunning, not quarrelsome, riotous or rowdy. They bear no ill-will or hatred, and they seek no revenge."[13]

To say "yes" to my neighbour, the system first has to be broken into, opened up. We have, in other words, to cease to believe in the system. The Virgin of Nazareth, the flesh, opens us to the spirit (otherness). Jesus said that we should "render to Caesar that which is Caesar's, and to God that which is God's (Mt. 22. 21). Like the prophets before him, he thus did not believe in Caesar, the flesh and the closed system. When Feuerbach and Marx said they did not believe in the "god" of Hegel and of the European bourgeoise (the only god they knew), they set out along the correct and orthodox path.[14]

To achieve the breakdown of the closed system of sin, otherness has to attack it subversively. The ana-lectic (what is outside the system), the absolute Other, the Word (in Hebrew *dābhār*, which has nothing to do with the Greek *logos*) breaks into the closed system and becomes flesh: "... in the form of God ... he emptied himself (*ekenosen*) and took the form of a servant"

---

[13] *Brevísima relación*, p. 33.

[14] See my paper "Atheism of the prophets and Marx," delivered to the 2nd Argentine Theologians Week, Guadalupe (Buenos Aires, 1973), and "Historia de la fe cristiana y cambio social en América latina," in *América latina, dependencia y liberación* (Buenos Aires, 1973), pp. 193 ff. There I show that the prophets begin their attack on the system of sin with a criticism of the idolatry and fetishism of that system. Would it not be both truly Christian to attack the fetishism of money (Marx, *Das Kapital*, I, chap. XXIV, 1: "Das Geheimnis der ursprünglichen Akkumulation")? Is it perhaps not correct that Hegelian theology should be denied in order to affirm instead an anthropology of the Thou (Feuerbach, *Grundsätze der Philosophie der Zukunft*), especially if we remember that Christ is the Other made man and mediator with God the Father and Creator? We might say that Latin American theology of liberation is non-believing when it comes to the religion of oppressionist Europe (not to confuse religion with Christianity: see my article, "From Secularization to Secularism", in *Concilium*, September 1969 (American edn., Vol. 47).

(*doulou*) (Phil. 2. 6–7). Christ, the Church, the prophet must assume within the system the position of the oppressed. The servant (*'ebhedh* in Hebrew, *doulos* or *pais* in Greek) really assumes the position of the oppressed, whether socially, politically, culturally or economically. In their alienated position they become like the Indian, African or Asian, the worn-out woman, the educationally manipulated child. They immerse themselves in the prison of sin (the system), but do not obey its rules.

The servant, the prophet or the poor in spirit[15] acting from amongst the ranks of and together with the oppressed, carry out the praxis of liberation (Hebrew *'abôdhāh*; Greek—*diakonia*) which is a work of righteousness and worship performed by the saving God. This service performed by the Samaritan or by Moses for the sake of the poor or the slaves as members of the outside, is a subversive praxis, both historical (and hence socio-political, cultural, economic and sexual) and eschatological. To this end he is called (Lk. 4. 18; Is. 61. 1) to undermine the system and direct history along a new path[16] and to liberate the poor in a year of festival or rejoicing.[17]

The liberator or the servant prophet, by responding to the cry of the poor (as other), discloses himself as the herald of the new system over against the old system of sin, imperialism and oppression, whether international or national, economic, political, cultural or sexual. Hence he announces the dispossession of the ruler and the end of him as an oppressor. The closed system or the flesh transforms mere domination into repression, violence and persecution. So the liberating servant is the first to die: "Jerusalem, Jerusalem! killing the prophets and stoning those who are sent to you!" (Mt. 23. 37). In such a case the liberator

[15] I may be permitted this translation of *hoi ptokhoi to pneumati* (Mt. 5. 3), to distinguish between the "poor" as the outsider (the sense in which I use it in § 5), and the "poor in spirit", i.e. the actively involved liberator, the prophet. See in my *El humanismo semita* (Buenos Aires, 1969), the footnote on "Universalismo y misión en los poemas del Siervo de Yahveh" (pp. 127 ff.).

[16] "He has put down the mighty from their thrones, and exalted those of low degree; he has filled the hungry with good things, and the rich he has sent empty away" (Lk. 1. 52–3). *Sub-vertere* in Latin is to make low what was high and vice versa.

[17] Lev. 25. 8–12 "Jubilee" comes from the Hebrew *yôbhēl*, the horn-shaped trumpet which announced the liberation of the slaves (Ex. 21 2–6).

becomes a redeemer—the one who, by a truly expiatory sacrifice (Hebrew—*kibburîm*), pays in his own flesh for the liberation of the other: "Whoever would be great among you must be your servant (*diakonos*), and he who would be first among you must be your slave (*doulos*); even as the Son of man came not to be served but to serve (*diakonesai*) and to give his life as a ransom for many" (*luton anti pollon*—Mt. 20. 26–8).

There are many examples of this praxis of liberation—the prophets and Jesus, the Christians persecuted under the Roman Empire, Bishop Valdivieso (murdered in 1550 by the governor for defending the Indians in Nicaragua), Pereira Neto in Brazil in 1969 or Mahatma Gandhi or Patrice Lumumba in the non-Christian Third World—we see how the liberator, when he announces the end of the old system, is assassinated violently and in cold blood by the angels of the Prince of this World, that is, by the conquistadors, the imperialist armies, the capitalist bankers or the "herodian" governments of the dependent nations themselves. The closed system spells death for itself. The death of the liberator is, on the other hand, the death of death and the beginning of a new birth (Jn. 3. 5–8).[18]

7. Towards an Ecclesiology of Redemptive Liberation

All the foregoing is constantly lived out in the actual historical context of the community of the "called", that is the Church or even world history itself.

Since the liberating and redemptive death of Christ, world history has been living under a new order of reality, since any man of good will receives enough grace for salvation. However, because of sin, historical institutions (social, political, economic, sexual and educational) tend to close in on themselves, petrify and become self-perpetuating. They have to be given new impetus, be opened to new influence and be given dialectical flexibility in the direction of the parousia. God, from the creative outside, has founded the Church at the very heart of the flesh, of the world, of the closed system (an alienating or kenotic movement). The Church, his gift, is the becoming flesh of the spirit.

[18] "That which is born of the flesh (the closed system) is flesh. That which is born of the spirit (the other, the outsider) is spirit" (*ibid.*).

By baptism, the Christian is consecrated to the liberating service of the world, and received into the community. The earthly phenomenon of the Church, an institutional community, was born, geo-politically speaking, in the western Mediterranean and reached maturity in Latin and Germanic Christianity, in other words in Europe, which together with the United States and Russia is the geo-political centre of our modern world. On the other hand, since it was born, socially speaking, among the oppressed people of the Roman Empire, it today finds itself part of those nations that oppress the dependent peripheral nations and frequently finds itself compromised with the ruling classes (at national level) or with the ruling culture.

Thus, the Church which has become flesh in the world (like the leaven in the dough in the parable) comes to be identified with the flesh and the closed system. This self-identification with the Prince of this World is the sin of the Church, which petrifies the system and even sanctifies it. The terms *Holy* Roman Empire, *Christian* countries, Western *Christian* civilization, and so on, bear witness to this.

But the essential nature of the Church as the liberating community and institution requires it to identify itself with the oppressed so as to "break down the barriers" of the systems which have become closed by the work of sin, or by injustice, whether political—at national or international level—economic, social, cultural or sexual. The sign (*semeion* of St John's Gospel) of the Church, its proclamation, can only be effected by involving the community in the movement of liberation (Hebrew—*pāsāḥ* means moving, march or flight), to move a system which acts oppressively towards becoming a new system which acts to liberate. And this, in its turn, is, so far as the Church is concerned, the sign of the eschatological forward movement of the Kingdom. The Eucharist is a foretaste, in the forward movement of the Kingdom; it is a feast of liberation from sin (from slavery in Egypt). The liberation of Latin America is, therefore, the compelling call to the Church in Latin America (a dependent and to some extent oppressed sector of the world Church). At the same time, liberation of oppressed classes—women, children and the poor—is also the basis of evangelization.

II. Application of the Theological Argument

We must now turn our attention to the theological argument itself, first of all as we see it in Europe. (We shall therefore be looking at what might be called the white theology of North America.) This may lead us to define the theology that emerges as a theology of oppression—whether applicable on a world-wide scale (coming from the peripheral nations), a national scale (coming from the oppressed classes), to sex (a theology of woman) or to education (from the point of view of the younger generation).

1. *Conditioning of Theological Thinking*

It is widely accepted by critical thinkers in Latin America today that all political expansion soon comes to be based on an ontology of domination (an *ad hoc* philosophy or theology). Modern European expansion had as its ontological foundation the *ego cogito*[19] preceded by the actual fact of "I conquer". For Spinoza, in his *Ethics*, the *ego* is a fragment of the unique substance of God—a position which the young Schelling and Hegel were to adopt later—the European *ego* had been deified. Fichte shows us that in the "I am that I am", the "I" is absolutely fixed.[20] It is an "I" that is natural, infinite and absolute (and in Hegel definitely divine). In Nietzsche, the "I" becomes a creative power ("I" as the "will to power"), while in Hüsserl it becomes the most abstract *ego cogito cogitatum* of phenomenology.[21] The most serious effect is that *the other* or the neighbour (the Indian, the African, the Asian or the woman) is reduced to the

---

[19] *"Je pense, donc je suis"* was a statement so firm and confident that the most determined contradictions of the sceptics were not enough to shake it;" see *Discours de la méthode*, IV (Paris, 1953), pp. 147-8.

[20] "Ich bin Ich. Das Ich ist schlechthin gesetzt" (*Grundlage der gesamten Wissenschaftslehre* (1794), § 1 (Berlin, 1956), I, 96). He still says that "the essence of critical philosophy is the absolute position of an 'I', absolute and unconditioned, and not to be defined in terms of any higher order." For the only translation in German: "Darin besteht nun das Wesen der kritischen Philosophie, dass ein absolutes Ich als schlechthin unbedingt und durch nichts Höheres bestimmbar aufgestellt werde). (*Ibid. I*, § 3; I, 119).

[21] See my *La dialéctica hegeliana*, 4-9 (pp. 31-121) and *Para una destrucción de la historia de la ética*, §§ 11-21 (Mendoza, 1972), pp. 75-162.

level of an idea. The meaning of the other is formulated in terms of the "I" who dreamed it into existence. The other is made a separate entity, becomes a thing, is abstracted into a *cogitatum*.

Similarly, European theology or the theology of the centre cannot escape from this reduction. The expansion of Latin-German Christianity gave rise to its own theology of conquest. Semitic and Christian thought of the Old and New Testaments was reduced to a process of Indo-European Hellenization from the second century onwards. Medieval European theology was able to justify the feudal world and the *ius dominativum* of the lord over the serf. Tridentine and Protestant theology had nothing to say about the Indian, the African or the Asian (except the Salamanca School and that only for a few decades). Finally the expansion of capitalism and neo-capitalism allowed Christians of the centre to formulate a theology of the *status quo* and the ecumenism of peaceful co-existence between Russia, the United States and Europe so as to dominate the "periphery" more effectively. The other—the poor—was once again defined in terms of the European "I": *Ego cogito theologatum*. With the basis of theological thinking so reduced, a parallel reduction occurs in the whole field of theology. Sin is reduced so as to apply only to *intra* national injustice; it is exclusivized, allowed to have no political application, shown to have nothing to do with sex (or at other levels, shown to have an excessive relation to sex). But more seriously the limits and meaning of salvation and redemption are equally reduced to the narrow bounds of the Christian experience of the *centre*. We have an individual salvation, interiorized and other-worldly, resorting frequently to some painful masochistic experience at a given time and place, whereas the true cross of real history demands our life at the least expected moment.

This theology suffers from many unconscious limitations. Firstly, the limitations of the religiosity of German-Latin-Mediterranean Christianity which was accepted without hesitation as real simply because it was Latin. Then there are liturgical limitations, in which the Latin-type liturgy is regarded as the only one acceptable for the Christian religion and which still prevents other cultures having their own liturgies. There are also cultural limitations, in that theology is the province of an intellectual élite, university professors in well-paid and secure posts, a situation far removed from, and unhelpful to the study of Tertullian and St Augustine. There are political limitations, for it is a theology adjusted and compromised by its closeness to the metropolitan power of the world. There are also economic limitations, for this theology finds favour for the most part among upperclass minorities in the bourgeoisie and in the neo-capitalist world (although sometimes there may be poor monks, they belong to "rich" orders). Finally, there are sexual limitations, because those who think theologically are celibates and have been unable to formulate an authentic theology of sexuality, marriage and the family. For all these reasons, modern European theology from the sixteenth to the twentieth centuries is unconsciously compromised by its connection with the praxis of oppression in the political, educational and sexual fields.

It would be no exaggeration to say that in many respects it is really a theological ideology in that many facets of it remain unseen by virtue of its origins, just as we are unable to see the further side of the moon simply because we are inhabitants of planet earth. And what is still worse, in Latin America there are many progressive theologians who simply repeat the theology of the centre and by so doing they obscure their own message and, to their shame, become just as much advocates of oppression.

2. Revelation and Faith—the Anthropological Epiphany

Western theology has for centuries taken certain presuppositions for granted as unquestionably correct. Kant's ontology (which postulates a rational faith), Hegel's (which sees faith as within the bounds of reason) or Heidegger's (the comprehensiveness of Being) admit the Wholeness of being as the only frontier of thought. Being-in-the-world is the fundamental fact, original and primary.[22] Existential theology starts from the basis of the

[22] The theology of Karl Rahner comes from Heidegger's philosophy (also influenced by Maréchal) and is set out in *Spirit in the World* (London and Sydney, 1968), or in *Hearers of the Word* (London and Sydney, 1969). Quite rightly Eberhard Simons, *Philosophie der Offenbarung. Auseinandersetzung mit K. Rahner* (Stuttgart, 1966), demonstrates that the *Mit-Sein*

world as the Whole. The fault lies in that, in fact, the Whole is always mine, ours, the European's or the centre's. What passes unnoticed is that I am thereby denying other Christian worlds and other equally valid experiences. I am denying anthropological otherness as a possible starting-point for theological thought.[23]

As the older Schelling so clearly saw in his *Philosophie der Offenbarung,* faith in the Word of the Other lies beyond onto-logical reason (the Hegelian *Sein*), an argument that Kierke-gaard carried forward (e.g. in the *Postscriptum*). Faith stands upon the revelation of the Other. Revelation is only the out-going message of God, existentially speaking, which sets out the guidelines for interpreting the reality of Christ. In everyday life (existentially),[24] God manifests the hidden secret (the fact of redemption in Christ) by means of an interpreting light (a classi-cist would put it: *ratio sub qua*), or by supplying guidelines (categories) for all mankind and for all history. God gives not only a specific revelation, but more importantly, the categories[25]

---

has not been brought out sufficiently in Rahner's thinking. It is not a matter of mentioning the other as a mere aside, but of making it the starting-point of theological argument, but not merely of the *divine* Other.

[23] For a philosophical point of view see the works of Levinas (*op. cit.*), and Michael Theunissen, *Der Andere* (Berlin, 1965), and chap. III of my *Para una ética de la liberación,* vol. I, pp. 97 ff.

[24] As Yves Congar so well shows, the *locus theologicus* is everyday events ("the history of the Church, in a certain sense, embraces all of it", see his "Church History as a Branch of Theology" in *Concilium*, September 1970 (American edn., Vol. 57). Revelation is mediated by historical other-ness—God reveals himself in history. In the same sense Edward Schille-beeckx, *Revelation and Theology* (London and Melbourne, 1967), offers us the "Word as the medium of revelation". However, in both cases, as with Schelling and Kierkegaard, the mediatory function of the anthropological outsider is not grasped. It is not enough to say that revelation is possibly effected in the form of human speech, as Rahner does in his *Hearers of the Word,* but we must go on to say that the poor, like the metaphysical other is the mediator chosen by God for his revelation. As a fact of history (not just of myth as in Exodus 3) Moses heard the word of God through the mediation of the poor (Ex. 2. 11–15), as Schillebeeckx says in his *Revelation and Theology.*

[25] These categories are flesh (Totality), the poor (the human outsider), God as creator and redeemer, the Word, the Spirit (outreaching modes of the divine in face-to-face encounter") and service ("ᵃbhôdhāh or dia-konia). See my *Caminos de liberación latinoamericana* II, VI. The category is what is revealed in Christ as essential revelation. What is interpreted by these categories is the Christian meaning of event, the fruit of faith.

which permit us to interpret it. Revelation comes to a peak in Christ with the New Covenant, but it unfolds its potentialities throughout the course of history. What we are trying to stress here is that this revelation is not effected in history by human words alone, but through man himself (as exterior to the flesh or the system), the poor and the Christ-man.

Faith, which accepts the Word of the Other, becomes Christian faith when the divine Word in Christ is accepted through the mediation of the poor man in history, who actually lives in a concrete situation. The true showing forth of the Word of God is the word of the poor man who cries "I hunger". Only the man who hears the word of the poor (beyond the system, and therefore ana-lectic, which presupposes that he does not believe in the system) can hear it as the Word of God. God is not dead. What has been assassinated is his self-manifestation—the Indian, the African and the Asian—and because of this God cannot reveal himself any more. Abel died in the self-deification of Europe and the centre, and therefore God has hidden his face. The revealed category is clear enough: "I was hungry and you gave me no food. . . . They also shall ask, Lord, when did we see you hungry?" (Mt. 25. 42–4).[26] Following the death of the "divine" Europe, there can rise the faith in the poor of the periphery, faith in God as mediated by the poor. The new manifestation of God in history (not a resurrection, for he never died) will be brought about by righteousness and not by endless theological treatises on the death of God.[27]

3. The Praxis of Liberation and Theology

Given the data of revelation and by virtue of living faith, theology is a reflection of reality. Recently there has been much talk of theologies of earthly realities or doubt, leading eventually

[26] In *Concilium*, February 1973 (American edn. vol. 82), much was said about liturgy, Scripture, poetry, but almost nothing about the privileged place of faith in the other—the poor; without him faith becomes ideology, mere doctrine, obscurity.

[27] See *Caminos de liberación latinoamericana* I, §§ 1–7; *Para una ética de la liberación latinoamericana*, §§ 31 and 36.

to a theology of revolution[28] or development.[29] In European circles, to take just the term political theology[30] the matter has sterner implications. But Latin America detects in the theologico-political argument an attempt to restrict the prophetic voice of protest to the narrow national sphere. From this narrow viewpoint the fact of international, imperialist injustice passes unnoticed. But eschatological, undiscriminating protest must reach out not only to the constituent parts of the system, but to the system as a whole.[31]

In the same way the provocative theology of hope[32] betrays the limitations of the critical theory of the Frankfurt School (which influences Metz) and the works of Ernst Bloch (who inspires Moltmann). Both these philosophical hypotheses have failed to overcome ontology and dialectic, and they consider the future as a development of the Self. Although Moltmann understands the future as otherness, he still has difficulty in finding beyond the projection of the system (but this side of the *eschaton*) an historical projection of political, economic, cultural and sexual liberation.

[28] From Latin America see Hugo Assmann, *Teología desde la praxis de la liberación* (Salamanca, 1973), pp. 76 ff. A bibliography on *Desarrollo y revolución*, CEDIAL, II, pp. 73–95. This idea and the one that follows are inspired in part by the Christian praxis in Latin America.

[29] Cf. Bibliography in CEDIAL (*op. cit.*), II, 31–47.

[30] The works of Johann Baptist Metz is of importance: starting with "Friede und Gerechtigkeit. Ueberlegungen zu einer 'politischen Theologie' ", in *Civitas* VI, (1967), pp. 13 ff.; then *Theology of the World* (London, 1969), and "The Problem of a Political Theology", in *Concilium* June, 1968 (American edn., Vol. 36); and finally the colourless "Erlösung und Emanzipation", in *Stimmen der Zeit* 3 (1973), pp. 171 ff. (where the word "Befreiung" is avoided in its ambivalent sense of "cross". The "cross" of the murdered prophet is not the same as the "pain" of the oppressed poor.

[31] Liberation protest as a function of the Church (see J. B. Metz, *Theology of the World, op. cit.*) is very different if it concerned with international political protest (pointing out the unjust acquisitiveness of the centre), and with social protest (pointing out the oppression of the ruling classes). In this situation we still look for a concrete programme of action to make the protest really mean anything. Theology is essentially an ethic, and most important, a political ethic.

[32] Cf. Jürgen Moltmann, *Theology of Hope* (London, 1969); *idem, Perspektiven der Theologie* (Mainz, 1968) and *Diskussion über die 'Theologie Hoffnung'* (Munich, 1967).

Hope extends as far as an historical change in the pattern of life,[33] but not to a radical renewal of the present system with a view to an historical liberation movement as a true sign of eschatological advance. Without this concrete mediation their hopes reaffirm the *status quo* and constitute a false dream.

On the other hand, a European theology of liberation will bring out clearly the question of Christianity and the class struggle,[34] but within the limits of a national Marxism and before moving on to the theory of dependence. It has not yet seen that the struggle of the proletariat within the centre itself, that is, in the metropolitan powers, can be oppressive in terms of the colonial proletariat of the periphery. Classes have been thinking double and may often oppose their own interests at international level. National liberation of the dominated countries goes hand in hand with the social liberation of oppressed classes. Hence the category known as the people takes on a special significance as opposed to the category of class.[35]

Latin American theology derives, by contrast, from the thinking of many politically involved Christians about the praxis for liberating the oppressed. This theology-ethic is a product of the periphery, coming from the outsiders, from the *lumpen* of this world. Their inspiration is not only sheer necessity (the existence within the system of matters needing attention), but also the desire to liberate (Hebrew *'abhôdhāh*; Greek—*diakonia*), that is a ministry of liberation beyond the limits of ontology. And the sphere of liberation is not only political, but also sexual and educational. In fact, this is a theology of the poor, woman as a sexual object and the child.

4. *Towards a Theology of Liberation*

After the great theology of Christianity from the fourth to

[33] See J. Moltmann, *Theology of Hope, op. cit.* Something in the nature of a reactionary professional ethic, but not a subversive movement to oppose the closed nature of the system, and which knows it has to initiate a programme of historical liberation as a sign of the coming Kingdom.

[34] Cf. Jules Girardi, *Christianisme, libération humaine et lutte des classes* (Paris, 1972).

[35] See my *De la dialéctica a la analéctica*, general conclusions (to be published in Salamanca, 1974).

the fifteenth centuries and modern European theology from the sixteenth to the twentieth centuries, the theology of liberation of the periphery and of the oppressed is in fact the whole of traditional theology set into redemptive motion from the point of view of the poor. The theology of Christianity (the old model) almost identified the Christian faith with Mediterranean Latin or Byzantine culture, subsequently halting progress. The argument over Latin in Vatican II itself is an obvious recent demonstration of this. Modern European theology, individualized and imperialistic, is reproduced in the colonies as progressive theology by those who operate as an oppressive colonial minority and take as the scheme of salvation a theology which for the periphery is meaningless and therefore uncritical. The *status quo* is once again supported. By contrast, the theology of liberation (where a theology of revolution is only a first stage, political theology is just one of the possible applications and the theology of hope looks to the future) is based on the praxis of liberation, or on the movement or way through the desert of human history, moving from sin as the dominating influence exerted by the various systems (political, sexual and educational) to irreversible salvation in Christ and his Kingdom (the *eschaton*). This movement is accomplished by everyman, all people and every age— in short, by the whole of human history. However, there are certain critical periods (*kairos*) in history and Latin America is living through one such period now,[36] when complete eschatological liberation can be more clearly indicated by the prophets, Christians or the Church. Thus the theology of liberation gradually becomes an African or black theology, though to date there has been no response from Asia,[37] and finally a theology of the whole world and of all the oppressed.

[36] Bear in mind that Latin America is the only continent, culturally speaking, which has been both Christian and colonial. Europe has been Christian, but was not colonized. Other colonial peoples have not been Christianized. This places Latin America in a unique position in world and ecclesiastical history. From our unique experience must come, of necessity, a theology which must be different to be authentic.

[37] In Africa, such authors as V. Mulango, A. Vanneste, H. Burkle; the "black theology" of J. Cone, A. Hargreaves, Th. Ogletree, Ch. Wesley point to this line of thought; see also J. Peters, "Black Theology as a Sign of Hope," *Concilium,* November 1970 (American edn., Vol. 59); G. D.

The theology of liberation which is coming from Latin American thinkers[38] can be distinguished when its dependence as a theology is realized in the same way as economy or culture is realized to be dependent (the culture of oppression as Salazar Bondy said in Peru in 1968). Gradually this theology discovers its own methods which I have defined as ana-lectic and not only dialectic,[39] in that it is listening to the trans-ontological voice of the other (ana-) and is interpreting its message by means of analogies. (The other, however, remains mysteriously distinct from us, until such time as the progress of the movement towards liberation allows us to enter upon its world). It adds an entirely new dimension to the question of analogies.

For its own part the theology of liberation favours the interpretation of the voice of the oppressed as the basis for its praxis. This is not a private departure within the unified Whole of universal abstract theology, neither is it an equivocal, self-explanatory theology.

Starting from a unique position of difference, each theologian, and indeed the whole of Latin American theology, takes a fresh

---

Fischer, "Theologie in Lateinamerika als 'Theologie der Befreiung' ", in *Theologie und Glaube* (1971), pp. 161–78; R. Strunk, "Theologie und Revolution", in *Theologische Quartalschrift*, 1 (1973), pp. 44–53; and CEDIAL, *op. cit.*, II, pp. 58–72). Some European opinions, for example, Vancourt, "Thélogie de la libération", in *Esprit et Vie* 28 (1972), pp. 433–440, & 657–62, who thinks that this theology is inspired solely by the Marxist method, are very biased.

[38] G. Gutiérrez wondered in his short work "Hacia una teología de la liberación" (Montevideo, 1969) whether beyond a theology of development we ought to formulate a specific theology of liberation. The previous year Rubem Alves in *Religíon: opio o instrumento de liberación?* (Montevideo, 1968) had already gone some way with this idea. Also Methol Ferré in his article "Iglesia y sociedad opulenta. Una crítica a Suenens desde América latina", in *Víspera* 12 (1969), offprint, pp. 1-24, points to a "struggle of two theologies", since "all theology one way or another has political implications", and in fact, "within the Catholic Church itself there exists oppression by the richer local churches of the poorer ones". Thus there arose a new theological argument.

[39] See my *Para una ética de la liberación latinoamericana*, § 36; vol. II, pp. 156 ff. I would define theology as *"an analectic pedagogy of historical and eschatological liberation"*. A pedagogy, for the theologian, is a teacher and not a politician, nor is he involved sexually; analectic because the method is neither purely epistemological nor dialectic. For this definition see my *Caminos de liberación II*, lecture XII.

look at traditional themes passed down through history, but enters the interpretative process from the distinct emptiness of his new found liberty (that is, with a blank sheet). The theology of a true theologian or a people like the Latin Americans is analogically similar, yet at the same time distinct, and hence unique, original and completely individual. If what is similar becomes univocal, the history of theology will remain European. On the other hand, if difference is made absolute, theologies become equivocal. The aim is not Hegelian identity, nor yet Jasperian equivocation, but analogy. The theology of liberation is a new focus in the history of theology, an analogical focus which has come to the fore after modern developments in Europe, Russia and the United States, and predating to some extent the most recent African and Asian theology. The theology of the poor nations, the theology of world-wide liberation is not easily acceptable to Europeans, who believe too passionately in their own invariable world-wide acceptance. They will not listen to the voice of the other (the barbarians, non-being if we define Being as the European way of thought), the voice of Latin America, the Arab World or South-East Asia and China. The voice of Latin America is no longer a mere echo of European theology. It is a barbarians' theology—as the apologists would say, making the contrast with the "wise according this world". But we know that we have taken up our stand on the further side of the modern, oppressive, European closed system. Our minds are set upon the liberation of the poor. We point towards the world-man of the future—man who shall be eternally free.

Translated by J. D. Mitchell

Gustavo Gutiérrez

Liberation, Theology and Proclamation

THEOLOGY is an understanding of the faith and a re-reading of the Word as it is lived in the Christian community. The ensuing reflection is orientated towards the communication of the faith and the proclamation of the good news of the Father's love for all men. To evangelize is to witness to that love and say it is revealed to us and made flesh in Christ.

The basis for discourse about the faith is midway between experience and communication. Theology is concerned with our being as men and as Christians, and is a function of the proclamation of the Good News. That is why it is a permanent yet ever-changing task. We have to get on with *being* Christians within an historical process that is transforming the conditions of human life all the time. The Gospel must be proclaimed to men who realize themselves as they work out their own destiny. Theological discourse concerns a Truth that is the Way; it is about a Word that is located in the midst of history. A task for all times, theology assumes different forms, depending on the Christian experience and the proclamation of the Gospel to men at a given moment of historical development.

Recent years in Latin America have been marked by the real, demanding discovery of the world of the other: the poor, the marginal, exploited class of society. In a social order which in terms of economics, politics and ideology was made by a few for their own benefit, the "others", that is, exploited lower classes, oppressed cultures, races subject to discrimination, are beginning to make their own voices heard. They are beginning to speak out directly and less and less through intermediaries, to rediscover themselves and make their unsettling presence felt in the system. They are increasingly less inclined to submit to demagogic manipulation or more or less disguised social assistance; instead they are gradually becoming the subjects of their own history and are forging a radically different society.

They can discover this only from within the historical process of liberation, which seeks to build a truly egalitarian, fraternal and just society. For some time now, a growing number of Christians have been sharing in the process of liberation, and through it, in the discovery of the world of the exploited and peripheral people of the South American continent. This commitment gives rise to a new way of being a man and a believer, of living and thinking the faith, of being called together in an "ecclesia".

This sharing of Christians in the process of liberation varies in radicalism and is virtually a process of searching and advancing "by trial and error". At times it gets bogged down at difficult points in the road, at others it moves forward at speed, thanks to some event or other. But it is following a path whose new significance for theological reflection and for the celebration in community of the faith is gradually becoming clear.

In this article I want to make a few observations about a theological task which begins from an historical practice of liberation, through which the poor and oppressed of this world are endeavouring to build a different social order and a new way of being men. This theological reflection is impelled by a desire to speak the word of the Lord to all men from that position of solidarity.

I. THE PRACTICE OF LIBERATION

The irruption of the other, the poor man, into our lives leads to active solidarity with his interests and his struggles. This commitment is expressed in an attempt to transform a social order whch breeds marginalization and oppression. Participation in the historical practice of liberation is ultimately the practice of love, the love of Christ in one's neighbour; and of encounter with the Lord in the midst of a conflictual history.

II. Who has been this Man's Neighbour?

Rediscovering the other means entering his own world. It also means a break with ours. The world of inward-looking absorption with self, the world of the "old man", is not only interior but is socio-culturally conditioned. To enter the world of the other, the poor man, with the actual demands involved, is to begin to be a "new man". It is a process of conversion.

Love for one's neighbour is an essential component of Christian existence. But as long as I consider as my neighbour the man "near me", the one I meet on *my* way, the one who comes to me seeking aid ("Who is *my* neighbour?"), my world remains the same. All individual gestures of aid, all superficial reform of society is a love that stays comfortably at home ("If they love those who love them, what reward will they have?"). If, on the other hand, I consider my neighbour as the man in *whose* path I deliberately place myself, the man "distant" from me, the one whom I approach ("Which of these three was neighbour *to this man?*"), if I make myself the neighbour of the man I seek out in streets and squares, in factories and marginal *barrios*, in the fields and the mines, my world changes. That is what happens when an authentic and effective "option for the poor" is made, because for the Gospel, the poor man is the neighbour *par excellence*. This option is the axle on which turns a new way of being a man and being a Christian in Latin America.[1] But the "poor" do not exist as an act of destiny; their existence is not politically neutral or ethically innocent. The poor are a by-product of the system in which we live and for which we are responsible. The poor are marginalized in our social and cultural world. They are the oppressed, the exploited, the workers cheated of the fruits of their work, stripped of their being as men. The poverty of the poor is not therefore an appeal for generous action to relieve it, but a demand for the construction of a different social order.

[1] Cf. texts of different sectors of the Latin American Church in *Signos de renovación* (Lima, 1969) and *Signos de liberación* (Lima, 1973). For an analysis of these texts see Ronaldo Muñoz, *Nueva conciencia de la Iglesia en América Latina* (Santiago de Chile, 1973).

It is, however, necessary to take one more step. The option for the poor and the oppressed through a liberating commitment leads to the realization that this commitment cannot be isolated from the social set-up to which they belong; otherwise we would not go beyond "being sorry for the situation". The poor, the oppressed, are members of a culture which is not respected, a race which is discriminated against, a social class subtly or openly exploited by another social class. To opt for the poor is to opt for the marginalized and exploited, to take stock of the social conflict and side with the dispossessed. To opt for the poor is to enter the world of the oppressed race, culture and social class, to enter the universe of their values and cultural categories. This means solidarity with their interests and their struggles.

The poor man is therefore someone who questions the ruling social order. Solidarity with the poor means taking stock of the injustice on which this order is built, and of the countless means it employs to maintain itself. It also means understanding that one cannot be *for* the poor and oppressed if one is not *against* all that gives rise to man's exploitation of man. For this same reason, solidarity cannot limit itself to just saying no to the way things are arranged. It must be more than that. It must be an effort to forge a society in which the worker is not subordinated to the owner of the means of production, a society in which the assumption of social responsibility for political affairs will include social responsibility for real liberty and will lead to the emergence of a new social consciousness.

Solidarity with the poor implies the transformation of the existing social order. It implies a liberating social praxis: that is, a transforming activity directed towards the creation of a just, free society.

III. History and Liberating Love

During the last two centuries man has begun to realize his capacity to transform swiftly and in a controlled manner the world in which he lives. That experience has changed the course of history and gives a definitive character to our age. Unsuspected possibilities have opened up for man's life on earth, but their appropriation for the benefit of a minority of the human race has provoked the frustration and exasperation of the dis-possessed masses.

The industrial revolution, as it was called, meant the begin-ning of a stage of broad and rapid production of consumer goods for man, based on a capacity to transform nature hitherto un-known.[2] The use of experimental science had already set in motion the attempt to dominate nature, but this mastery was only to reach full consciousness and maturity when scientific knowledge was translated into a technique of manipulation of the material world, and into the possibility of satisfying the vital needs of man on a large scale.[3] The productive powers of man increased beyond foreseeable limits and brought about a revo-lutionary change in the economic activity of society. The process has continued, and advances spirally, and we are today in the middle of what is called a second industrial revolution. All this has given contemporary man the consciousness that he is capable of modifying his living conditions radically, and has given a clear and stimulating affirmation of his freedom vis-à-vis Nature. It has also produced the widest-ranging differences among the peoples of the earth that history has ever known.

One of the most uncontrolled consequences of the industrial revolution was the progressive displacement of man by the machine. This created a marginal social surplus in the course of the production of wealth: the so-called "reserve industrial pool" consisting of a growing mass of marginalized people not reabsorbed by the system. The nineteenth century was slow to take account of this social price for the accelerated rhythm of industrialization and its corresponding technological boom. Furthermore, as technical progress became more and more re-fined, and the standard of living of the developed countries rose, the process was accompanied by an international division of labour which produced those vast differences between one country and another.

Therefore, whereas the industrial revolution has given modern man a unique situation and power to transform nature, it has

[2] Cf. Eric Hobsbawm's classic work, *The Age of Revolution: Europe 1789-1848* (London, 1962).

[3] In its early stages the industrial revolution received some impetus from the inventive work of artisans. Shortly after that it made dynamic pro-gress following scientific advances.

also sharpened contradictions in society until a situation of international crisis has been reached which forceful measures can no longer hide.

These consequences of the industrial revolution make for a better understanding of the extent of another historical process, whose origins go back to the same period and give evidence of another aspect of man's transforming action. We refer to the political field, which experienced in the French Revolution the practical working of the possibility of a profound transformation in the existing social order. It declared the right of every man to share in the conduct of the society to which he belongs. Neither the immediate results of the French Revolution nor the largely declaratory character of that proclamation are our concern here. The important thing to note is that, with all its ambiguities, that event put an end to one kind of society, and from then on the people as a whole aspired to share in political power effectively and adopt an active role in history: in short, they aspired towards a truly democratic society. As in the previous instance, we are faced here with a new affirmation of man's freedom, this time in relation to social organization. But for the democratic organization of society to be real it is assumed that just economic conditions exist; if these do not exist within the underdeveloped countries, or in their external relations with the developed countries, explosive tensions occur in national and international contexts.

The contemporaries of those events in their opening stages were acutely conscious of being on the threshold of a new historical era marked by critical reason and man's transforming liberty.[4] All this was to lead, they thought, to a different man, more master of himself, and of his destiny in history. History could no longer be thought of with nature divorced from society. The industrial revolution and the political revolution were in fact to appear more and more clearly, not as two processes

[4] Cf. reflections on the Kantian Enlightenment in his *Philosophy of History* and of Hegel in his *Lessons on the Philosophy of History*. On this subject cf. the classic work of Ernst Cassirer, *The Philosophy of the Enlightenment* (New York & London, 1959), and the more recent work of W. Oelmuller, *Die unbefriedigte Aufklärung* (Frankfurt, 1969). For a theological view consult, J. B. Metz, J. Moltmann, W. Oelmüller, *Kirche im Prozess der Aufklärung* (Mainz, 1970).

which happened to be contemporary or convergent, but as two movements depending one on the other. As both advanced, their reciprocal involvement became more evident. To transform history required a simultaneous transformation in nature and society. In this transforming praxis, there is more than a new consciousness of the meaning of economic and political action—there is a new way of being man in history.

To speak of a transformation of history from the standpoint of dominated countries and marginalized men, the poor of this world, leads us to see this as a liberating praxis. This means seeing in it something which is perhaps missed when it is viewed from the standpoint of the minority of the human race, who control the major part of scientific and technical assets and also political power in the world today. That is why a liberating praxis has a subversive look about it: that is only natural, in a social order where the poor man, the "other" of this society, is only just beginning to be listened to.[5]

What is really at stake is not a greater rationalization of economic activity or a better social organization, but through them the whole question of justice and love. The terms are classical and perhaps little used in strictly political language, but they recall for us the human reality at the heart of the matter. They remind us that we are speaking of men, of whole peoples who are suffering poverty and despoliation, who cannot exercise the most elementary human rights, who scarcely know they are men. That is why a liberating praxis, in so far as it starts from authentic solidarity with the poor and the oppressed, is specifically a practice of love: real love, effective and historical, for men of flesh and blood. Then love of our neighbour is love of Christ, who is identified with the very least of our brothers. Any attempt to separate the love of God from the love of our neighbour gives rise to attitudes which impoverish the one or the other. It is easy to set a "praxis of heaven" against a "praxis of earth" and vice versa: easy, but not in accord with the Gospel of God made man. Therefore it seems more genuine and profound to speak of a practice of love which is rooted in the gratu-

[5] For the political options now being followed in Latin America by this liberating praxis see my *Theology of Liberation* (New York, 1973; London, 1974), chapters 6 and 7.

itous, free love of the Father, and which makes itself history in solidarity with the poor and dispossessed, and through them in solidarity with all men.

IV. Believing and Understanding

Commitment to the process of liberation, with all its political demands, means taking on the world of the poor and the oppressed in a real and effective manner. This sets up a new spiritual requirement at the very heart of the liberating praxis. I mean the matrix of a new theological reflection, of an intellection of the Word, the free gift of God, breaking into human existence and transforming it.

The praxis of liberation must lead one to become poor with the poor. For the Christian committed to it, this will be a way of identifying oneself with Christ, who came into the world to proclaim the Gospel to the poor and liberate the oppressed. Evangelical poverty thus began to be lived as an act of liberation and love towards the poor of this world, as solidarity with them and protest against the poverty in which they live; as identification with the interests of the oppressed classes and a rejection of the exploitation of which they are the victims. If the ultimate cause of the exploitation and alienation of man is egotism, the underlying motive of voluntary poverty is love for one's neighbour. Poverty—the results of social injustice, which has its deepest roots in sin—is accepted, not in order to make it an ideal of life, but in order to witness to the evil it represents. The condition of the sinner, and its consequences, were accepted by Christ, not to idealize them, but out of love and solidarity with men, and to redeem them from sin; to fight against human egotism and abolish all injustice and division among men. Consequently, the witness of poverty lived as an authentic imitation of Christ, instead of separating us from the world, places us at the very heart of the situation of despoilment and oppression, and from there proclaims liberation and full communion with the Lord. Spiritual poverty is proclaimed and lived as a way of being totally at God's disposal, as a spiritual childhood.[6]

All this means entering a different world and outlines a

[6] The theme of evangelical poverty is dealt with more fully in *Theology of Liberation, op. cit.,* ch. 13.

Christian experience as yet untried, full of possibilities and promise, but with no lack of twists and blind alleys on the route ahead. There is no smooth, triumphant highway for the life of faith. Absorption in the political demands of a liberating commitment can lead to difficulties. The tensions of living in solidarity with exploited people who belong to a Church containing many members on the side of the prevailing social order, can cause some to lose the dynamism of their faith and suffer the anguish of a dichotomy between their Christian existence and their political action. Crueller still is the case of those who see their love for God vanish in favour of a love which he himself has inspired and nourished; the love of man, a love which, unable to observe the unity demanded by the Gospel, remains heedless of the plenitude God contains in himself.

Such cases exist. To be present in the frontier areas of the Christian community, where the revolutionary commitment is at its most intense, is not a tranquil experience. The clues to any solution can only arise from the depths of the problem itself. Protective measures conceal reality and delay any useful response. They also display a neglect of the urgency and gravity of the reasons which lead to a commitment to men exploited by a cruel, impersonal system, and finally they show a lack of belief in the strength of the Gospel and of faith.

In reality a liberating commitment now means for many Christians an authentic *spiritual experience*, in the original, biblical sense of the term; a living in the Spirit which makes us recognize ourselves as freely and creatively sons of the Father and brothers of man ("God has sent into our hearts the Spirit of the Son who proclaims Abba, Father"). In Christ we become simultaneously and inseparably sons and brothers ("Whoever sees me sees the Father; whoever does the will of my Father, he is my brother"). Only through concrete acts of love and solidarity will our encounter be effective with the poor, with the exploited man, and in him our encounter with Christ ("... you gave it to me"). Our denial of love and solidarity will be a rejection of Christ ("... you refused it to me"). The poor man, the other, reveals the totally Other to us. This is what is involved, life in a presence of the Lord, at the centre of an activity in one way or another related to the political world, with its confrontation of interests and conflicts and the need for a level of scientific rationale to understand it in its complexity. To paraphrase a well-known saying, we need "contemplatives in political action". We are unused to this. A spiritual experience seems to us something encountered well away from human realities of such marked lack of purity as political action. The specific form of our insertion in the realities of politics will depend on our situation in society and in the church community. However, that is where we are going, towards an encounter with the Lord not in the poor man "isolated and good", but in the oppressed man, fighting ardently for his most elementary rights and for the construction of a society in which men can live as men. History is the scene of the revelation God makes of the mystery of his person. His word reaches us in the measure of our involvement in the evolution of history.

To opt for the poor man, to be identified with his lot, to share his destiny, means a desire to make of history genuine brotherhood for all men. It means accepting the free gift of sonship and opting for the cross of Christ in the hope and joy of his Resurrection.

In these concrete conditions the process of conversion occurs, the nodal point of all spirituality. Conversion means going out of oneself, being open to God and others; it implies a break, but above all it means following a new path.[7] For that very reason, it is not an inward-looking, private attitude, but a process which occurs in the socio-economic, political and cultural medium in which life goes on, and which is to be transformed. The encounter with Christ in the poor man constitutes an authentic spiritual experience. It is a living in the Spirit, the bond of love between Father and Son, God and man, man and man. Christians committed to an historical praxis of liberation try to live this kind of profound communion. They find the love of Christ in their encounter with the poor and in solidarity with them: they find faith in our situation as sons of the Father working for a society of brothers: and they find hope in the salvation of Christ, in commitment to the liberation of the oppressed.

All this is a unifying experience which all too often is im-

[7] Cf. R. Schnackenburg, *L'existence chrétienne selon le Nouveau Testament,* vol. I (Paris, 1971), p. 35.

poverished when an attempt is made to express it. This may be due to its handling by theologians who tend to separate and even set at odds the elements of this experience; or it may be due to the defensive attitude adopted against Christian sectors who see in the commitment to liberation a challenge to their privileges in the present social order. The Christian experience involved is not without risk of being subject to *simpliste* identifications and distorting reductions; but it is a bold and profound attempt to live in Christ by taking on oneself the history of suffering and injustice of the poor of this continent. To the extent that this experience has managed to achieve genuine expression and free itself from a mediatized language, its contribution has begun to show fertile possibilities for the whole ecclesial community.

V. Understanding Faith

At the root of all theology is the act of faith. It is not there as a simple intellectual adhesion to the message, but as a warm welcome of the gift of the Word heard in the ecclesial community; as an encounter with the Lord, as love for our brother. Faith concerns Christian existence taken as a whole. To welcome the Word, to make it life, a concrete act, is the starting-point for the intellection of faith. That is the meaning of St Anselm's *"Credo ut intelligam"*, as he has expressed it in his celebrated text: "I do not try, O Lord, to penetrate your depths, because my intelligence could not conceivably attain that; but I wish to understand to some extent your truth, which my heart believes and loves. I do not seek to understand so as to believe, but *I believe in order to understand,* since I am sure that if I did not believe, I would not understand" (Proslogion, end of the first chapter).

The primacy of God and the grace of faith give theological work its *raison d'être*. Beginning from that, it can be properly grasped that if the Christian seeks to understand his faith it is ultimately as a function of the "imitation of Christ", which means thinking, feeling and acting like him. An authentic theology is always a spiritual theology, as the Fathers understood it. The life of faith is not only the point of departure, it is also the point of arrival for the task which theology sets itself. Belief and understanding are part of a circle.

Theology always employs a certain rationale, even if it does not identify with it. This rationale corresponds to the cultural universe of the believer. Every theology asks itself about the meaning of the Word of God for us in the present in history, and attempts at a reply are made as a function of our culture and of the problems which face men of our time. From the standpoint of this cultural universe we reshape the message of the Gospel and the faith for our contemporaries and ourselves.

That is what Thomistic theology, for example, attempted, boldly using Aristotelian philosophy and the whole world vision to which it was tied. This was a step of first importance in the understanding of faith. Today we are witnessing a crisis in the rationale classically employed in theology. The matter has been amply studied and its causes precisely indicated, and no purpose would be served by going into further detail about it here. Among the results of this situation is the philosophical eclecticism which is one of the features of a certain contemporary philosophy. Another result is the efforts which we see, not so much to rebuild an impossible unitary theological system, but rather to find new ways towards the reformulation of the Word.[8] In a more radical manner perhaps, it has provoked questioning in the field of the theory of knowledge,[9] an area not perhaps given sufficient attention in theological thinking, but certainly requiring consideration. On what assumptions does theology base its approach to historical reality? What is the influence on our theological reflection of the place held by the ecclesial institution in present-day society? Or, to use a common expression nowadays, where does the theologian speak from? For what and for whom does he speak? These questions have opened a

[8] For a broad view of these questions and of current paths in contemporary theology consult the valuable reflections of C. Geffré in *Un nouvel âge de la théologie* (Paris, 1972). See also H. Bouillard, "Exegèse, herméneutique et théologie, problèmes de methode" in *Exegèse et herméneutique* (Paris, 1971); and the precise analysis of J. P. Jossua, "Ensemblement du discours chrétien" in *Christus* (June 1973), pp. 345–54.

[9] See J. Guichard's attempt to highlight these questions in "Foi chrétienne et théorie de la connaissance" in *Lumière et Vie* (June–August 1973), pp. 61–84.

major consideration which always crops up when one stage is closing and another beginning: what is meant by making theology?

An important role in these queries is played by scientific knowledge, especially when history or psychology is touched upon. The sciences are forms of expression of human reason; they reveal to us aspects of nature and man which evade other approaches to these realities and therefore cannot be neglected by theology. Philosophical reflection, even when opening up new paths, preserves all its validity and is enriched in permanent dialogue with the sciences. It responds to questions which do not belong to the domain of the sciences, and it makes its own contribution to the knowledge of history and to the role of the free, creative action of man. This complexity and wide-ranging character of human knowledge is set to work in the historical praxis of liberation, and contributes to make it more effective. It is also present in any discourse on faith which is attempted from a position of solidarity with the poor and the marginalized.

Much contemporary theology seems to start from the challenge of the *non-believer*. He question our *religious world* and faces it with a demand for profound purification and renewal. Bonhoeffer took up the challenge and put the incisive question which is at the root of many theologicial endeavours nowadays: how is God proclaimed in a world which has become adult? This challenge in a continent like Latin America does not come primarily from the man who does not believe, but from the *man who is not a man*, who is not recognized as such by the existing social order: he is in the ranks of the poor, the exploited; he is the man who is systematically and legally despoiled of his being as a man, who scarcely knows that he *is* a man. His challenge is not aimed first at our religious world, but at our *economic, social, political and cultural world*; therefore it is an appeal for the revolutionary transformation of the very bases of a dehumanizing society. The question is not therefore how to speak of God in an adult world, but how to proclaim him as a Father in a world that is not human. What is implied in telling this man who is not a man that he is a son of God? To some extent these were the questions put by Bartolomé de las Casas and many others in the sixteenth century on the basis of their encounter with the American natives. The discovery of the other, of the exploited, led to a reflection about the demands of faith which contrasted with that conducted by those who sided with the rulers, Ginés de Sepúlveda, for example.

Today the historical framework is different, the social analysis is another one, but we are witnessing the rediscovery of the poor man in Latin America. Solidarity with him means deliberate entry into the arena of history, into confrontation between countries and between social classes. It means entry on the side of the dominated and oppressed. However, the social system it-self, which creates and justifies this situation, is not really ques-tioned unless a share is taken in the efforts to transform it radi-cally and forge a different order. Localization in the praxis of liberation means taking on what we called the complexity and wide-ranging character of human knowledge; ultimately it means entering a different cultural world.

From within this cultural world in which we are situated due to our involvement in the Latin American historical process, we try to reformulate the Gospel message. From this viewpoint discourse on faith will necessarily follow a different path from that presented to it when the challenge of the non-believer is taken as the starting-point. Theology will be a critical reflection from and about the historical praxis of liberation in confronta-tion with the Word of the Lord lived and accepted in faith. It will be a reflection in and about faith as a liberating praxis: an intellection of faith made from an option; a reflection based on a commitment to create a just, fraternal society, and with a duty to contribute to make that commitment fuller and more radical. The theological discourse becomes truth (is veri-fied) in its real, fecund insertion in the process of liberation.

To reflect on the faith as liberating practice is to reflect on a truth which is made, and not just affirmed;[10] it is to start from a promise which is fulfilled throughout history and at the same time opens history up beyond itself. In the final instance the exegesis of the Word, to which theology wishes to contribute, is accomplished in deeds. This factor, not mere affirmations, will

[10] Note in this perspective the reflections of Duns Scotus on theology as a practical science. Cf. also the work of Frans v.d. Qudenrijn, *Kritische Theologie als Kritik der Theologie* (Munich-Mainz, 1972).

rescue the understanding of faith from idealism of whatever kind.

VI. Evangelization and "Ecclesia"

Insertion in the liberating process constitutes a profound and decisive spiritual experience at the very heart of the historical commitment, with its necessary political implications. As we have already remarked, this is a source of knowledge and energy for a way of theologizng which opens up new perspectives.

We are not faced here with new fields of application of old theological notions, but with the provocation and necessity to live and think the faith in different socio-cultural categories. This has occurred at other times in the history of the Christian community and has always produced fears and anxieties. In this search, we are impelled by the urgency to pronounce the Word of the Lord in our everyday language.

This is the point at issue; a re-reading of the Gospel message from the standpoint of liberating practice. Theological discourse operates here as a mediator between a new manner of living the faith, and its communication. If we accept that theology is a re-reading of the Gospel, this is carried out with a view to the proclamation of the message.[11]

To know that the Lord loves us, to welcome the free gift of his love, is a profound source of joy for the man who lives by his Word. To communicate that joy is to evangelize: it means communicating the Good News of the love of God, which has changed our lives, and communicating it freely, as the love which originated it was freely given. The task of evangelization always starts from an experience of the Lord: a living out of the love of the Father, who makes us sons and transforms us by making us more fully men and brothers of men.

To proclaim the Gospel is to proclaim the mystery of sonship and brotherhood, a mystery hidden from all ages and now revealed in Christ.[12] To proclaim the Gospel therefore means to

[11] Y. Congar, a theologian with a profound ecclesial and pastoral sense, has often emphasized this link between theology and proclamation. See, e.g., *Situations et tâches de la théologie* (Paris, 1967).

[12] "Sonship is *the* distinctive feature of the Kingdom of God, the sole, true one": from J. Jeremias, *Théologie du Nouveau Testament*: vol. I, *La prédication de Jésus* (Paris, 1973), p. 227.

call people together in an "ecclesia", to unite them in an assembly. It is only in a community that faith can be lived in love; only there can it be celebrated and deepened; only there can it be lived in one single gesture, as fidelity to the Lord and solidarity with all men. To accept the Word is to convert the Other into others, the rest. We live this Word with them. Faith cannot be lived on its private, inward-looking plane because faith rejects all turning in upon oneself. In the dynamism of the good news which reveals us as sons of the Father and brothers one of another, is the creation of a community, of the Church, which will be a visible sign before men of liberation in Christ. This proclamation of the Gospel calling us together in an "ecclesia" is made from an option of real, active solidarity with the interests and struggles of the poor, of the exploited classes. To try to take up this "place" means a deep break with the way of living, thinking and communicating the faith in the Church of today. All this demands a conversion to another world, a new style of intellection of the faith; and it leads to a reformulation of the message.[13]

In this reformation, what has come to be called the political dimension of the Gospel takes on a new face. It is seen more clearly than before that there is no question of adding on something from outside the Gospel by yielding to partisan pressures of our age, but that we are in the presence of what is necessarily an offshoot of the Gospel. Moreover, the political dimension is accepted frankly and openly. Its precise extent has still to be defined, and any simplistic view of it must be avoided, but no claim to be outside politics can obscure an evident reality or weaken a conviction that is growing firmer all the time. The gift of sonship is lived in history. By making men brothers, we welcome this gift, not in words but in deeds ("Not all who say to me Lord, Lord, will enter the Kingdom of Heaven, but he who does the will of my Father"). To struggle against all injustice, despoilment and exploitation, to be committed to the

---

[13] "The biblical hermeneutic will differ according as we consider the God of the Bible as totally distinct, with nothing in common with the universe in which man is so profoundly integrated, or simply as the Other 'whose ways are not our ways' (Is. 55. 8), nor his thoughts our thoughts, but yet 'We are indeed his offspring' (Acts 17. 28)." Cazelles, *Ecriture, Parole et Esprit* (Paris, 1970), p. 76.

creation of a more brotherly and human society, is to live the love of the Father, and witness to it. The proclamation of a God who loves all men equally must be given substance in history and must become history. To proclaim that love in a profoundly unequal society marked by injustice and the exploitation of some peoples by others, of one social class by another social class, will make this process of "becoming history" a conflict-laden, interpellating experience. That is why we said that the political dimension is inside the dynamism of a Word which seeks to become incarnate in history. The demands of the Gospel are incompatible with the social situation which is being lived in Latin America, with the ways in which relations between men operate, with the structures in which these relations are found. More is required than the rejection of some individual injustice or other; we are faced with the need for a different social order. Only a certain degree of political maturity will permit a true political understanding of the Gospel and will prevent it from being reduced to an aid programme, however sophisticated, or to a simple task of "human promotion". It will also avoid the reduction of the evangelizing task to a form of political action with its own laws and demands.

The authentic proclamation of the love of God, of brotherhood and of the radical equality of all men, to the exploited man of our continent, will make him see that his situation is against the Gospel, and this will help him to take stock of the profound injustice of this state of affairs. The oppressed sectors will acquire a clear political consciousness only by direct participation in the struggles of the people; but in the complex totality of the political process which must break with an oppressive social order and lead to a brotherly society, the ideological struggle holds an important place. In Latin America, the whole "Christian set-up" is made to play a part inside the dominant ideology, which helps to strengthen and affirm a society divided into antagonistic classes. Conservative sectors in fact frequently appeal to Christian ideas to justify the social order which serves their interests and maintains their privileges. That is why the communication of the message re-read from the standpoint of the other, of the poor and oppressed, will serve to unmask any attempt to ideologize the Gospel and justify a situation contrary to the most elemental demands of the Gospel.

VII. Liberating Evangelization

Are we faced with a political reductionism of the Gospel? While wishing to escape from one ideological use of Christianity, are we not falling into another? The danger exists and it would be ingenuous and dishonest to deny it. It needs to be kept constantly in mind.

The re-reading of the Gospel from the standpoint of solidarity with the poor and the oppressed enables us to condemn the way those in power fetter the Gospel in order to place it at the service of their own interests. We cannot do this properly, if we are not aware of the permanently creative and critical nature of the liberating message of the Gospel. This message is not identified with any social form, however just it may appear to us at the time. The word of the Lord interpellates every historical achievement and sites it within the broad perspective of the radical and total liberation of Christ, the Lord of history. A relapsing into ideology made to justify a particular social situation is inevitable when the Gospel is not lived as the word of a Father who loves us freely and gratuitously, with a love which renews the face of the earth, and calls us always to a new life in his Son.

The liberation of Christ is not reduced to a religious plane tangential to the concrete world of men, as those who wish to domesticate the gospel claim. The salvation of Christ is in fact so full that nothing escapes it. Evangelization is liberating because it is a message of total liberation which necessarily includes a demand for the transformation of the historical and political conditions in which men live. But this is only to be grasped in all its profundity when it is known that this liberation leads this same history beyond itself, to a fullness which is beyond the reach of anything that can be foreseen or done by human beings.

While the men who are the objects of the Gospel message are not abstract, a-political beings, but members of a society marked by injustice and the exploitation of some men by others, the Christian community from which the message is proclaimed and which most of these men belong to in one way or another, is not a reality outside history either. Its past and present link it closely to the history of the Latin American people from their early days. Without historical perspective, it is not possible to grasp what is involved in evangelizing nowadays a people to whom the message has been proclaimed already and forms a part of their lives in one way or another. On the other hand, without taking into account the situation of a Church which for the most part is tied to the social order which is being lived in Latin America, no one can grasp what is implied by the liberating character of that evangelization. Those historical and political kinds of conditioning must be analysed and detailed in order to put into correct focus the proclamation of the message in the Latin American situation.

VIII. Solidarity with the Poor and the People of God

The proclamation of the Gospel from the standpoint of identification with the poor, summons the Church to solidarity with the lower classes of the continent, solidarity with their aspirations and struggles to be present in Latin American history. The Church is called to contribute from its own task, the proclamation of the Gospel, to the abolition of a society built by and for the benefit of a few, and to the construction of a different social order, juster and more human for all.

This process leads to profound breaks and re-orientations in the Church of today. They will not, however, be fertile if they only express personal anguish, a crisis of identity, emotional reactions or impatience, however legitimate all this may be. This road leads only to defensive attitudes, authoritarian measures, gestures inspired by fear or by the search for security, and the endless spiral of conflicts inside the Church. Breaks and reorientations must be radical, must go to the very root of the matter, which in this case extends beyond the narrowly ecclesiastical ambit. The root lies in the way of being a man and a Christian in the present of the Latin American reality; that way consists of identification with the oppressed classes of this continent of injustice and despoilment, which is also a continent of thirst for liberation and hope.

This assumes that there are new experiments in the task of

evangelization and convocation into an "ecclesia".[14] There will be different ways of being present in the world of the people, beyond all institutional rigidity. We will have to be prepared to listen to a different voice from the one we are accustomed to hear in the Church. There must be critical awareness of the social and cultural categories which imprison our way of living and proclaiming the Gospel, and make it alien to the world of dominated peoples, marginated races, exploited classes; and even contrary to their profound aspirations towards liberation. It also assumes an authentic search for the Lord in this encounter with the poor, and a lucid explanation of what that spiritual experience signifies.

What is envisaged in this view is the creation of Christian communities in which the private owners of the goods of this world cease to be the masters of the Gospel; communities in which the dispossessed can bring about a social appropriation of the Gospel. Such groups would prophetically proclaim a Church wholly at the service of men in their battle to be men; a creative and critical service always, because rooted in the Gospel. This struggle for manhood follows a way difficult to understand from the old world in which the Word has been and still is lived, thought and proclaimed. Only by putting down roots among marginated, exploited men and by rising from among these men themselves, from their aspirations, interests, struggles, cultural categories, will a people of God be forged which will be a Church of the people, which will cause *all* men to listen to the Gospel message and will be a sign of the liberation of the Lord of history.

None of this would have meaning or could even be glimpsed if it were not already outlined, albeit timidly, in trials now going on in various parts of the continent. These attempts start off from the insertion of a growing number of sectors of Christians —workers, professional men, peasants, bishops, students, priests —in the process of liberation in Latin America. Their insertion is official, and is called to greater profundity and to experience, clarification and purification: it is called to take its place freely and critically within any simplifying political process which fails

---

[14] Cf. Karl Rahner's perspicacious and courageous remarks on a Church of the future in *Strukturwandel der Kirche als Aufgabe und Chance* (Freiburg, 1972).

to take into account all the dimensions of man. It is called to grow, so that the voice of the Christian people of the lower sectors is heard in their own language. There are difficulties in this insertion: the terrain offers hard going at times, with hostility and resistance from those, whether Christians or not, who are tied to the old order of things. But it is a real commitment and is beginning to reveal its fecundity for the liberating option, for an understanding of the faith and for a proclamation of the Gospel.

The times which are being lived through in Latin America do not allow of any euphoria. The spirituality of the Exodus is no less important than that of the Exile. The joy of the Resurrection requires first death on the Cross—and this can take differing forms. But hope is always there. The situation which is being lived in the continent perhaps makes us live and understand in a renewed form what Paul called "to hope against all hope".

Translated by J. P. Donnelly

Leonardo Boff

Salvation in Jesus Christ and the Process of Liberation

I. A New Parousia of Jesus Christ as Liberator

EACH generation brings a new *parousia* of Christ because in each age he is given a new image, the result of the difficult synthesis between life and faith. The true Jesus is not really the Jesus of history. All that has been said and done with regard to the person and message of Jesus through the centuries is part of the mystery of Jesus, the definitive shape of which is still being formed. Only at the end of history will we know who Jesus Christ really is and was.

Today, in the experience of faith of many Christians in Latin America, he is seen and loved as the liberator. The process of liberation taking place throughout the continent affords a hermeneutic context for the elaboration of a new image of Jesus Christ. It originates, on the one hand, in the concrete praxis of liberation and, on the other, in the desire for an effective liberation which, despite all the failures, is still seen as a real possibility. Every day it becomes more and more clear that the real problem in Latin America is an under-development, involving a degrading cultural, political, economic and also religious dependence. Liberation is then seen as a setting in motion of a process which will lead to freedom. This process of liberation can be divided into liberation *from* an overall system of oppression and liberation *for* the self-realization of the people, enabling them to determine for themselves their political, economic and cultural destiny.

Christians have learnt a great deal from taking part in this process of liberation. They have learnt first of all that Christian praxis is not enough and that it is first necessary to discover already existing Christian elements, even when the movement is led by men without explicit faith. They have also concluded that it is naïve to identify ecclesiastical action at the level of praxis with Christian action, because the Christian message had frequently been manipulated to legitimize the *status quo*. The Churches in Latin America have been on the side of the holders of power and therefore on the side of the oppressors. At the same time there is the new hermeneutic possibility, revealing liberating aspects of Christ which would otherwise have remained concealed. In every century Christians have read texts concerning the Kingdom of God, Jesus' conflict with the Pharisees and the text of Luke 23. 2 about Jesus subverting the people. But their situation has not allowed them to hear the political echoes of these words. Today, for many Christians of Latin America these texts have acquired an immediate political and existential significance. Their concentration on the liberating aspect has resulted in a new image of Jesus Christ and enormous possibilities for the praxis of liberation.

II. READING ABOUT CHRIST IS NOT DESCRIPTIVE BUT HERMENEUTICAL

Our object is to emphasize the liberating dimension of Jesus Christ as it emerges in the Christian experience in Latin America. It is not enough simply to read about the figure of Jesus purely in the light of his *ipsissima vox et facta* and within the apocalyptic framework and the sociological background of his time. Exegetes, using more and more sophisticated methods, have done this and their work is very valuable,[1] but it is not a science

---

[1] See the principal Latin-American works; H. Borrat, "Para una cristología de la Vanguardia" in *Vispera* 17 (1970), pp. 26–31. A. Zanteno, *Liberación social y Cristo* (Cuadernos Liberacion, ed. Secretariado Social Mexicano 1971); G. Gutiérrez, "Christ and Complete Liberation" in *A Theology of Liberation* (Maryknoll, N.Y.), pp. 168–88: F. Barvo, B. Catao, J. Comblin, *Cristología y pastoral en America Latina* (Santiago, Barcelona 1965). H. Assmann, *Teología desde la praxis de la liberación* (Salamanca, 1973), pp. 57 *et seq.*: L. Boff, *Jesus Cristo Libertador* (Petrópolis, 1972).

in itself. It possesses a function within a systematic, thorough comprehension of the texts, but in itself it can even prevent access to the central structure of the Christian message. The elements that give permanent validity to this message, above the pressures of history, can only be adequately grasped in a hermeneutic approach. From this, the *ipsissima intentio Jesu* emerges, revealed but also veiled by his words and actions.

In other words, it is not enough to know in detail what is meant by the Kingdom of God to Judaism and to Jesus himself. It is not enough to elucidate the contemporary or apocalyptic background, with all the elements it gave impulse to—the coming of the Son of Man, the resurrection of the dead, the coming of the new era and so on. We must seek a hermeneutic reply to certain questions. What is conveyed by the term Kingdom of God? What does this aim to express at its deepest level? What is the apocalyptic message? A correct hermeneutic approach will show us that both the Kingdom of God and the apocalyptic aspect are in the service of a greater reality which was not fully expressed in the earlier understanding even though it was based on a study of Jesus Christ himself. A deeper vision will help us to perceive that this greater reality, expressed by Jesus under the sign of the Kingdom of God, is identical with that which is expressed in the theology of liberation within the differences of time, space and language. The same identity is expressed here and now under another logos which both reveals and conceals.

To deal specifically with the central message of Jesus about the Kingdom: what is the hermeneutic meaning of this?

III. The Kingdom of God as a Total Structural Revolution

The Kingdom of God expresses man's utopian longing for liberation from everything that alienates him, factors such as anguish, pain, hunger, injustice and death, and not only man but all creation.[2] The Kingdom of God is the term used to convey

---

[2] See the exegetic works dealing with this theme: R. Schnackenburg, *God's Rule and Kingdom* (London and New York, 1968); H. Flender, *Die Botschaft Jesu von der Gottesherrschaft* (Munich, 1968); W. Knorzer, *Reich Gottes* (Stuttgart, 1969); J. Bonsirven, *Le règne de Dieu* (Aubier, 1957); Boff, *op. cit.*, pp. 62–75.

the absolute lordship of God over the world stricken and oppressed by diabolic forces. God is now going to come out of his silence and is going to declare: "I am the meaning and the future destiny of the world! I am total liberation *from* all evil and liberation *to* all that is good!" With this expression Kingdom of God, Jesus makes a radical statement about human existence, its principle of hope and its utopian dimension. He promises that it will no longer be utopia, the object of anxious expectation (cf. Lk. 3. 15) but topia, the object of happiness for all the people (cf. Lk. 2. 9). Therefore the first word of his message is, "The time has come, and the Kingdom of God is close at hand. Repent, and believe the Good News" (Mk. 1. 14).

The Kingdom of God is not only spiritual, but also a total revolution of the structures of the old world. Hence it is presented as good news for the poor, light for the blind, healing for the lame, hearing for the deaf, freedom for those in prison, liberation for the oppressed, pardon for sinners and life for the dead (cf. Lk. 4. 18–21; Mt. 11. 3–5). It follows that the Kingdom of God is not the other world, but *this* world transformed and made new.

Have not all men dreamt, sleeping or waking, yesterday, today and always, of such a utopia? Was this not the dream of the Old Testament, firstly as a land flowing with milk and honey and later as a new heaven and a new earth (cf. Is. 65. 17; 66. 22)? Did the deliverance from Egypt not foreshadow the definitive liberation (Is. 11. 11, *et seq.*; Mt. 2. 13, *et seq.*)? Did total reconciliation not include the cosmos with its animals and its powers (Is. 11)? God's love of men is compared to the love of the mother for her child (Is. 49. 15; 66. 13), to the love of the father for his son (Hos. 11. 1) and to the love between wife and husband (Hos. 2. 19). Is this not the promise of a future, more profound love, when God will dwell among his own, will be their king (cf. Mal. 3; Zeph. 3. 15) and finally will be all in all (1 Cor. 15. 28)? The Kingdom of God which Christ preaches is to be the realization of this hope: "For men it is impossible, but not for God" (Mk. 10. 27) through Jesus Christ.

The Apocalypse with its bizarre world-vision is intended to witness to the eternal optimism which is the essential message of all religion, that God will have pity on this unhappy world, which will reveal its total meaning and its radical perfectability, if acted on by God himself.[3]

When we say that the Kingdom of God expresses man's utopian longing, we do not mean to convey the idea that the Kingdom is a mere organic extension of this world, as it is encountered in history. The Kingdom does not evolve, but breaks in. If it were the evolution of present possibilities, it would never surpass the situation of the present, which is always ambiguous, with the wheat and the darnel growing together. But the Kingdom of God means precisely revolution in the structures of this world, with the world being preserved as the place where God reveals his glory. The Kingdom is therefore the presence of the future within the present.

IV. The Temptations of Jesus—Regionalization of the Kingdom

The Kingdom of God represents the totality of the world in God. The temptation is to regionalize it and particularize it down to one political model, one ideology of the common good or one religion. Jesus himself was confronted with similar temptations, as the evangelists tell us (Lk. 4. 1–13; Mt. 4. 1–11) —the temptation of the Kingdom as political or religious domination and miracles satisfying all man's needs, including hunger.[4] These temptations (as Lk. 22. 28 suggests) beset Jesus throughout his life. They correspond exactly to the three models of King and Messiah which his contemporaries expected (king, prophet and priest). They all point to the reduction of the totality of the Kingdom to one particular province of this world. Jesus overcame these temptations, not trying to have a fourth model accepted, but living in a continuous and permanent relation with the Father. What the Father commands is the way he follows, whatever it may be. He gives up all desire for personal power, and allows himself to be led by the will of the Father, as revealed

---

[3] Cf. H. H. Rowley, *The Relevance of Apocalyptic* (London, 2nd edn., 1947). J. Schreiner, *Die alttestamentlich-judische Apokalyptik. Eine Einführung* (Munich, 1969), pp. 195 ff.

[4] P. Hoffmann, "Die Versuchungsgeschichte in der Logienquelle. Zur Auseinandersetzung der Judenschristen mit dem politischen Messianismus" in *Biblische Zeitschrift* 13 (1969), pp. 207-223.

to him in his encounter with the tensions and conflicts of the situation.

It is worth noting that in all his attitudes, whether in the moral disputes with the pharisees, or the temptation to power formulated by the apostles themselves, Jesus refuses to impose norms or solutions which might regionalize the Kingdom. He keeps it totally open and he maintains this totality on the basis of his experience of God the Father, who offers salvation to all indiscriminately, the good and the bad (cf. Mt. 5. 45), and especially to those who consider themselves alienated from God. His universal message of the Kingdom stands as a radical criticism of the religion of his time, and sets off a conflict which ends in his death because of his refusal to make the Kingdom of God fit the pattern expected by the Jews. This insistence on preserving the total character of the Kingdom does not lead Jesus to do nothing or just to hope for the coming of the new order. On the contrary, he creates a new attitude in the presence of concrete human realities, unmasking their self-sufficiency. He does not base his criticism on a utopian Kingdom, but inaugurates a new praxis which anticipates in a specific form the new world that is hoped for.

V. A New Praxis of Jesus as Liberator of the Consciousness of the Oppressed

One of the characteristics of the behaviour of Jesus was certainly non-conformity. This is clear from his words ("You have heard what was said in former times...") and his actions within prevailing social and religious order.[5] The gospels show that Jesus was a sign of contradiction (Lk. 2. 34), pointing to a crisis in Judaism (Jn. 7. 43; 9. 16; 10. 19). He confronted the heartless casuistry of the rites of purification (Mk. 2. 27), matrimonial legislation (Mk. 10. 11–12) and the use of power (Lk. 22. 25–28). He submitted the Old Testament law and prophets to the demands of love and freed the creative imagination from the burden of its own past. He did not aim at novelty in what he said. His parables in the arguments with the Pharisees showed

[5] J. Ernst, "Der Nonkonformismus Jesu" in *Anfänge der Cristologie* (Stuttgart, 1972), pp. 145–58.

that he wanted his hearers to understand. That is why he appealed to their reason and not to authoritarian norms. His praxis liberated through the new solidarity which he established with those who were oppressed by the system. These were the people who did not know the law and thought themselves condemned (Jn. 7. 49)—women and children, tax collectors, the practitioners of despised trades (shepherds, barbers, etc.), the afflicted and the public sinners. Christ openly took their part and was called a friend of sinners and of the collaborators with the Romans, a glutton and wine-bibber (Mt. 11. 19; Mk. 2. 14–17).

To those who were scandalized he narrated the parable of the prodigal son (Lk. 15) or simply said: "I did not come to call the virtuous, but sinners. . . . It is not the healthy who need the doctor, but the sick" (Mt. 9. 13).

His sovereign disregard for class differences, his welcome to a prostitute, his conversation with heretics (the Samaritan woman), his close companionship with a collaborator of the Romans (Mk. 2. 15–17), a zealot guerrillero (Mk. 3. 18–19) and with enthusiastic aspirants to the power of the Kingdom (Lk. 9. 46) show that he broke down barriers and brought about liberating communication among men. Masters and slaves were brought into brotherly relationships of mutual service (Mt. 23. 8–10; Mk. 10. 42–44). His demands must not be read within the context of the law, because his gospel does not set out to be a more perfect kind of pharisaism. On the contrary, he criticized all forms of legalism. He taught and showed in his life that the law commands but love saves. The law is there for human use and is purely functional (cf. Mk. 2. 27). When he taught love as the supreme norm for human relationships, he rejected any self-enclosed system of norms and he radically criticized all fetishism and all subservience to a social or ecclesiastical system.

This new praxis of Jesus Christ is the Kingdom itself already present. He showed himself to be a free man. He was himself the best personal example of the Kingdom. His existence was one of total reconciliation, even within his conflicts with the pharisees, because he rejected none and welcomed all: "Whoever comes to me, I shall not turn him away" (Jn. 6. 37).

This liberating praxis of Christ was not born of a humanitarian spirit, but of a profound experience of God, who seeks out the prodigal son and the lost sheep, a God of absolute goodness, love and forgiveness. This God gives himself to all without discrimination, to the pious and to sinners. Because he turns to man, man must turn also to his fellow man. Everything must serve this—worship, prayer, sacraments and Church, because the sacrament of the brother is the principal sacrament of salvation (Mt. 25. 31–45; Lk. 10. 29–37). Jesus lived his experience of God. He loved all men and especially the socially and religiously alienated.

The Kingdom of God signifies all this. It is, moreover, not already complete, but it has been inaugurated. It is present and already among us (cf. Lk. 17, 21; 11. 20) in Jesus himself and in the new praxis which he initiated and which is open to the future. The parables of the yeast (Mt. 13. 33), of the seed placed in the earth (Mt. 4. 26–29), of the darnel and the wheat (Mt. 13. 24–30) and of the dragnet of good and bad fishes (Mt. 13. 47–50) speak of the future which is nevertheless fermenting in the present. There is no separation between present and future, but a process of liberation, and the break-through of the Kingdom which is now near (Mk. 1. 14). These attitudes of Jesus point to the liberation, now in progress, of the consciousness of the oppressed. They keep a permanent value for the faith, which overcomes in this way any tendency to iconize the figure of Jesus, depriving his historical actions of their liberating meaning.

VI. Death and Resurrection—A Paradigmatic Reality of the Process of Liberation

The death and resurrection of Christ, as well as being the major events of the mystery of Christ and of the Christian faith, possess an intrinsic relation with the Kingdom. The Kingdom preached by Christ is the total good news for all creation. It concerns not only politics and religion, but the totality of man's experience. This cosmic character of the Kingdom provoked a crisis in Judaism which culminated in the rejection of Jesus.

The cross is the symbol of what the world can do, with its piety (pious people, not bad people, condemned Jesus), with its zeal for God and with its dogma and its revelation, understood as self-sufficient models. The cross is a paradigm of a set of priorities based on self-sufficency, and organized as a power or

religion. These involved the rejection of the future, of the Kingdom as the totality of liberation and of Jesus as the forerunner
and bearer of this liberation. Jesus made no compromise. Faith-
fulness to the Kingdom led him to accept, not without fear and
trembling, death and the cross. The cross did not reveal the
failure of Jesus, despite his inability to convince anyone of the
truth and possibility of the Kingdom as complete liberation. It
possessed a more profound (and therefore more permanent)
logos, which with Jesus was expressed in an exemplary, eschatological fashion.

The structure of sin was given historical form as the human
will to power, the spirit of vengeance, the rejection of God as
the future and fixation on the past and the present created and
domesticated by man. The cross was the real symbol of the
kingdom of man. It therefore appeared to Jesus, who always
lived on the terms of the Kingdom of God, as repugnant and
totally absurd (Heb. 5. 7). Accepting the cross with courage, he
transformed it into a sign of liberation from the very elements
that had forced it on him—the spirit of vengeance, divisions,
self-sufficient turning-in on oneself—and he created the possibility of true liberation, of communion, of love. With the cross,
Jesus conquered the greatest temptation of his whole life, the
temptation to use power as a means of enthroning the Kingdom.

The Kingdom of God is not the subjection of men either to
religion or to politics. That would always fragment the Kingdom and make it merely partial. But the Kingdom happens
when man leaves the security of his past and gives himself up to
the future of God, or the God of the future. Hence the Kingdom
of God is only inaugurated when conversion occurs, which means
leaving room for God, emptying oneself and experiencing an
exodus. Jesus on the cross lived out a similar annihilation of all
desire for effective results and all certainty of triumph. The cross
meant total abandonment (cf. Mk. 15. 34) and therefore the
complete emptying of self which opens the way to the fullness
of God in human reality.

Christ's resurrection shows what happened in his emptying himself in death the total self-communication of God. It is the parousia
of the Kingdom proclaimed, and the epiphany of the future
promised. The Kingdom was realized in the person of Christ

crucified in a definitive, eschatological form. Resurrection, therefore, is not a return to the structures of the old world, where
death reigns, sin flourishes and the darnel coexists with the
wheat. It is the implosion or explosion of the new heaven and
new earth with the new Adam (cf. 1 Cor. 15. 45). Hence resurrection means liberation to divine *and* human fullness, towards
a complete realization of man and the cosmos in God. It is the
utopia of the Kingdom transformed into an "evento-topia".

With the cross as with the resurrection, an event takes place
in an eschatological form, which is not exclusive of Jesus, but
which happens every time the Kingdom of God breaks into the
kingdom of men. That is, resurrection occurs as an experience
of liberation, when elements of oppression are overcome and the
shell which had been enclosing new life is broken open. The
experience of new and future events, not manipulated by man
(although new and future elements in human life are an anticipation of this potential future and novelty) means a resurrection, which in Jesus was transformed into a definitive event,
an example to the whole remaining process of liberation.

With death and resurrection, the presence of the total liberation, which is no longer a process or a hope, but an event of
divine and human joy, is celebrated. From this, impulse is given
to the process of liberation, which, in the pain of its birth, groans
for historical realization.

VII. Salvation in Jesus Christ in the Liberation in Latin America

The totality of salvation present in the dead and risen Christ
does not exempt faith from working towards the concrete historical fulfilment of the Kingdom. This does not fall from
heaven, but breaks in from the latent, radical quality of the
present moment. There is therefore continuity between the
Kingdom of God and the kingdom of man. Faith does not proclaim another world, but a *new* world. It will not, however, be
complete, because the kingdom of man is also the kingdom of
the Antichrist and the darnel. "On this earth the Kingdom is
already present in mystery" (*Constitution on the Church,* 39).

It is not found in its totality, but in its historical mediations, and it is in the process of formation at all the levels of reality—political, economic, social and religious.

The Church is not the only bearer of the Kingdom. It is proclaimed whenever there is a real human growth in justice, in the defeat of oppression and in the establishment of a wider realm of freedom. Understanding this, we need to beware of those who would neglect the present for the sake of the future of the Kingdom, as if the future did not depend on what we do now. The present is intimately bound to the eschatological future, because the present is one form, although a defective one, of future achievement in historical mediations.

In Latin America this means that the effort made throughout the whole continent towards freedom from economic, political or cultural oppression is not merely a political imperative. It is rather a demand of faith—faith which has become praxis, not a drug to keep the non-conformists doped. It is the way the Kingdom of God is encountered in our lives. Oppression by the ruling order, prison, torture, the loss of fundamental liberties of expression—this is experiencing the cross in everyday existence. The cross is taken up, not stoically as a burden which we cannot get rid of, but as an essential element to the paschal experience of liberation. This attitude gives suffering a special meaning. It is a way of sharing in the deprivation experienced by millions of people, whose humiliation and affliction are the historical, anonymous and present reality of the passion of Christ.

What must be done in the light of salvation in Jesus Christ cannot be deduced from the evangelical model or from the model of Jesus Christ. Liberating salvation is not a model, a specific, universally valid statement expressed by Jesus Christ. That is not the level at which specifically Christian activity operates, because the way ahead is always indicated by concrete circumstances and corresponds to the time and place of each situation. Jesus followed the path of the prophet-martyr. This was the road which within his situation God the Father asked him to follow. In this life, the specifically Christian dimension appeared and is an example for all which must be present in all concrete models, no matter how widely they diverge from one another—renunciation of the desire for revenge, disinterested love, universal forgiveness and continued reference to the mystery of the Father. The radical, practical living of this dimension means that we proclaim Jesus of Nazareth as the Christ, the Lord and the present Kingdom. This dimension gives the Christian praxis its Christian character, whatever the concrete historical form it takes —whether as the exercise of political power or the struggle to achieve it.

A temptation which is common to Christians is the tendency to justify their praxis with a gospel text or an action of Jesus. They appeal to violence because Jesus made use of it (cf. Jn 2. 15–17). Non-violent action is acclaimed because Jesus preached it and lived it (cf. Mt. 26. 52; 5. 39). Both approaches envisage specifically Christian action within a determined model, and therefore in a false hermeneutic position. Christian faith does not prescribe a specific concrete programme but demands a specific attitude which must be present in any practical action or any position taken. Therefore, if Christians aim at taking power because this appears to them to be the imperative of the moment, they must do so not as domination but as service and not in a spirit of vengeance but as a reconciliatory solution to discrimination in social structure. This attitude is the achievement of Christianity. If other Christians renounce power and preach non-violence, because the situation demands this, they do so in the same evangelical spirit as the group already mentioned, by incarnating in this way the feelings of Christ himself (Phil. 2. 5) about selflessness and fraternal service.

The Kingdom is achieved within the process of liberation. They are not identified, because the Kingdom is an eschatological totality. But precisely because of that it is encountered in history and gives meaning to history as an anticipation of full liberty and a promise of future fulfilment. In what Assmann has called the "intense and urgent times"[6] which Latin America is living through, the total liberation of Jesus Christ is mediated by an attempt to free oppressed, underdeveloped men and to make them more human and by the growing solidarity and participation of the great majority. All this is more aspiration than reality, it to become reality and not just a wish, faith must commit Christians

[6] Cf. H. Assmann, op. cit., pp. 171–202.

(because of their faith) to concrete engagement in the liberating praxis.

VIII. Faith is not Ideology but a Source of Functional Ideologies

The process of liberation, in order to maintain its purely Christian character, implies acceptance in its praxis of the Paschal experience. In other words, it must die to its own models and its own conquests. On the one hand, it must embrace them with great zeal, because they constitute the Kingdom which is present in the ambiguities of history, and on the other hand, it must die to them because they are not the whole liberation or the whole Kingdom. With its death, it makes way for the resurrection of other concrete formulations which will mediate the Kingdom, and so it "makes ready the material of the celestial realm" at the same time as it realizes a "foretaste of the world to come" (*Constitution on the Church*, 38, 39).

When the faith assures us that the future of the world is guaranteed by the full liberation of the risen Christ, it does not give us, as many Christians mistakenly believe, the key to all political and social enigmas. The Christian, like other men, still has to seek and struggle for the conquest of power without giving way to the ambition to dominate and still has to endure repression without any spirit of vengeance. He must also recognize that Christianity, precisely because it is not an ideology, does not offer him a concrete model of liberating action, valid for now and always.

The gospel encourages us to use the creative imagination to elaborate ideologies, both on the basis not of a total *a priori* scheme, but of an analysis the present situation and in the service of a liberating project. With this in mind, the Christian must not be afraid to take a concrete decision and risk failure. This decision may well be an historical mediation for the coming of the Kingdom. That is why he must earnestly pray every day: "Thy Kingdom come!"

What the concrete shape of that decision will be, the Christian cannot know *a priori*. What he can do is be attentive to the call of the situation itself, and see there what is the incarnation which the eschatological Kingdom requires to be assumed, either through a dangerous acceptance of power or by way of critical collaboration in prevailing models and either by receding into the catacombs or by prophetic, liberating actions capable of awakening the dormant consciousness. In all these attitudes, full of uncertainty and ambiguity, the authentic Christian faith can be realized. It can also be perverted if the course adopted is based on narcissism, or a retreat into a closed, self-assured mentality.

Translated by J. P. Donnelly

Joseph Comblin

Freedom and Liberation as Theological Concepts

ESSENTIAL Christianity isn't just talking about God or the love of God. It's making the love of God and the love of man come together. No one has stated that coincidence as uncompromisingly as Jesus Christ and made it the central point of his message —the light which makes every other part absolutely clear.

Nor is Christianity a matter of announcing a "state of grace" or the "raising of man to a supernatural state." All religions say that. Instead, for a Christian, that elevation to a "supernatural order" or "participation in the divine" must coincide with the restoration of "natural" man. In Christianity a man can become a son of God only in being a real man. Man rediscovers his human existence and acquires his divine being by doing one and the same thing. No one has stated that coincidence as radically as Christianity.

But as soon as it starts thinking about Christianity the human mind tends to dissociate what Jesus joins together. Theologies tend to separate what the Gospel unites, and in so doing destroy the very object they claim to be examining. They study the love of God and the love of man, or grace and freedom, as separate phenomena. The tragedy of any Christian theology is that in trying to master intellectual methods it runs the risk of being mastered by them. In fact such methodologies are made in order to study the love of God or human relations, supernatural states or religious messages, and various earthly realities, as separate things. They are not designed to conceive of unity. Whenever it allows the techniques it uses (linguistics, philosophy, the humanities) to dominate, theology divides and isolates. And that alone means that it ceases to be Christian.

The real object of Christian theology is to keep in mind and deepen that mysterious unity between the love of God and the love of one's neighbour wherever it's in danger. Theology is critical if it submits to the measure of that unity all the analyses and intellectual constructions it uses or submits to. It has to put all aspects of its message under the spotlight of the unity of the two kinds of love. Apart from that unity, Christian themes necessarily drop to the level of a gnosis or a law (in the biblical sense of the word).

What I have just said helps in understanding what has happened in the history of theology to the message of freedom and liberation. In the Bible and in Christian tradition there is a message of liberation which has been lost in theology. It's split off, and when it's split it's done for. What Christianity says about freedom now doesn't let through anything of the original message. The practice of theology has obscured the object of theology.

There is a theological tradition which studies freedom within a problematical complex of relations between God and man. It is concerned with the question of grace and freedom within justification. There is another theological tradition which includes freedom among the conditions for a moral action. Yet another tradition emphasizes the "freedom of the Church" as against civil society. And another states the limits of freedom when faced with authority within the Church itself. Each of these traditions—freedom and grace, freedom and necessity, freedom and power, freedom and law or authority—develops in accordance with an appropriate methodology so that, ultimately, the message of freedom disappears entirely. What the Gospel asserts, theology ignores: Jesus' debate with the Pharisees; the central theme of his message, the coming of the Spirit and of freedom according to Paul, John's "the truth will set you free".

Yet this biblical message exists. It is borne by a living tradition which theologies cannot express. There is a ferment of freedom and of liberation of social man, primarily in religious and monastic tradition (a conception of life among men, rather than a form of asceticism or mysticism), in medieval communal life and in modern social Catholicism. In the life of these movements there is much more of it than theological treatises would have us believe. An authentic form of critical theology consists in bringing out what spontaneous theologies hide of the living essence of the Gospel because the methods that they use aren't designed to display it. The self-alienation of theology is clear in that ultimately it doesn't acknowledge Christianity and its cause in the liberation movements of the modern—the contemporary—age, because they don't accord with any of the problems peculiar to the theological treatises: hence they don't seem to accord with Christianity. But theology has suppressed the point of convergence from which it should examine the Christian message throughout its entire historical development. Today the basic theological problem is to rediscover the point of synthesis and to fight unremittingly against all those secularizations which leave human reality to the "experts".

I. History of Freedom in Christian Theology

1. *Grace.* An important area of theology opened up with the Pelagian controversy. It occupied far too large a space in history: grace and freedom, nature and supernature, Protestantism, Jansenism, Molinism, and so on. The themes of freedom and liberation were absorbed. For centuries there were attempts to define the conditions for compatibility between grace and freedom— the two seemingly irreconcilable and yet unavoidable principles of justification. How could freedom be affirmed without destroying grace, and vice versa? A major part of the problem of modern atheism prolongs this very line of thought. In this perspective, God and freedom limit one another mutually in a certain way, or at least it is a question of making them seem not to restrict one another, and yet to restrict one another.

But in Christianity this problem is not only secondary but ultimately insignificant and only obscures Jesus' message of freedom. For centuries theologians have disputed a question which hid the essential.

In fact the matter of Christianity is how grace frees, how it remakes freedom, and what this freedom actually is. The field of human freedom is social life. Man is free "with" other men and in his relations with them. He is free in his action with them on nature. Therefore it is a question of revealing the connection between the Spirit and this field of freedom: that is the object of the Christian message. The rest is relatively gratuitous philosophical speculation. Theology has let itself be drawn on to ground chosen by the Pelagians—that of individual asceticism and the affirmation of a freedom of solitude and withdrawal into the self. The Pelagian concept of freedom was not put in question.

This tradition also concentrates the entire discussion on a formal question: the formal constituent of the act of justification. Freedom is one of the conditions for choosing salvation. The content of freedom is still outside the question. The doctrine of the two kingdoms is almost implicit here. Human freedom is a human quality at the point of entry into the supernatural order. It isn't surprising that here this freedom of justification seemed alien to the social problems of our age, so that no one thought of making the connection. The Church's social teaching developed in a perspective of social order and justice based on a natural order, and justification surrendered even the name of liberation. The biblical message of freedom had disappeared: no one needed it any longer: why not forget it? And the liberation movements proceeded under the dominance of an historical reason alien to Christianity.

2. *Human actions.* Traditional theology allowed freedom a share in human actions. How was responsibility (essential to sin and salvation) to be reconciled with Greek intellectualism? How could contradiction be avoided? Where was freedom to be located in the process of human action considered in a Greek perspective? Scholastic theology found a place for it, but located it in a problematics which did not allow the constituents of the biblical message on salvation to develop. The meritorious action as defined by traditional theology remains a strictly individual action, and freedom is an attribute of the individual. It is impossible for freedom to appear as a mode of communal life. It is neither an acquisition nor a process, but something given.

The freedom of human action also remains alien to struggles for "political liberties." No distinction is made between the

freedom of the slave and that of the master, as if the Christian
message had nothing to say on that subject.

Perhaps the course of scholastic theology would have been
quite different if Aquinas had come across Aristotle's *Politics*
earlier on. But he discovered it too late for the political perspective to force him to rearrange his entire problematics of man
and freedom. His successors did not dare (and were not able)
to start all over again in a political perspective; if they had done
so, perhaps they would have referred to the forgotten biblical
message.

3. *Social teaching.* The theme of the "freedom of the Church"
has been a traditional one since Constantine and developed in
the context of the struggle between the two powers, outside the
other sectors of theology. As far as the internal life of the Church
was concerned, there the topic of freedom was set against that
of authority and the authority-freedom duality was most often
treated outside the biblical message of liberation. Because of inter-
ference between the authority-freedom relationship in the Church
and in civil society, the problems of political and social freedom
were generally examined on the basis of a problematics of order
and justice and, in this case too, without any connection with
the biblical message, which certainly seemed of no value.

It was with Maritain that comparisons began to be made between Christian social teaching and its theological message. But
even Maritain did not really succeed in making the link: he
kept the distance between the two planes: that of a spiritual
ascent towards God by means of a "spiritual" freedom that
was properly "supernatural" and that of earthly struggles for
those political "freedoms". God and one's neighbour remained
in different if parallel sectors, and contacts between them were
still secondary.

In short, theological science allowed itself to be channelled off
by the problems and methodologies of the Platonic ascent of the
soul (and related religious philosophies), by Aristotelian meta-
physics, by law and by the philosophy of right: the message of
liberation was obscured, and vanished into treatises prepared in
advance.

II. The Biblical Message

The controversy about hermeneutics is in progress. It is a matter of knowing how to proceed from the "biblical sciences" to a Christian theology, and how to read the Bible in a "Christian" way. Most of those biblical scholars who dare to face the problem believe they can get out of it by condensing biblical themes into a kind of religious message addressed to a non-temporal area of interiority. But precisely that kind of biblical message is without biblical foundation. The hermeneutical problem focuses on the spiritual interpretation of Scripture. For the sense intended by Jesus himself cannot be de-temporalized. It can be revealed only in time: that is, in actual human contexts, stages in an uninterrupted evolutionary process. The Bible does not refer to a non-historical area of man, but to the means of entering into relation with others and with nature. It refers to the means of making history, and assumes the historical responsibility of man.

If the actual human condition and the actual course of history were to be surrendered to a pure scientific rationality, Christianity would lose its meaning. We would have to acknowledge that biblical language was clearly pre-scientific. Its value would be reduced to that remnant that the sciences have as yet been unable to assimilate. In reality, faith in the word of God expressed in the Bible implies that there is, beyond all scientific specialisms and beyond all scientific "rationalisms", a vision of man to be found in what is most basic, in what is within the reach of the unpretentious, and at a level of primary evidence or of radical understanding which can be apprehended only by a simple vision. Biblical language is that of the ordinary, non-expert, who achieves a clarity about man and his destiny which no science can replace.

The Bible supposes that human destiny cannot be entrusted to the experts, but that it is the task of all men to think it out and take it up. That is why the biblical message refers to all human problems in all their implications and ramifications—including all questions treated by scientific rationalism, though on a distinctive plane. Hermeneutics consists in marking out that plane.

The biblical message of freedom is not to be found only in those texts which speak explicitly of freedom. We have to start from the general context of the people of God and all the themes which relate to it: covenant, city of God, justice, power and domination.

The range of these themes is not apparent if we are content to attribute them to a Church conceived as a sect or religious institution. Judaism reduces the people to the synagogue and gnosis to a sect of initiates. In fact these themes define a new way of being man, an anthropology which subjects to criticism both the anthropologies of the present and those of the past. Man in the Bible lives his life, like Jesus, in interdependence with others, or the totality of men. The biblical people are a collective responsibility. Freedom consists in a mutual responsibility in which each man is responsible for all and for the very development of that collective responsibility. The biblical man denies the separation between a public life which would be the domain of a class or a caste predestined for government and domination, and the mass of individuals confined to a private life. The people are a way of communal life. It is impossible simultaneously to acknowledge the true God and to break the social pact of which he is the guarantor.

Undoubtedly the "sciences" tend to denounce the mythic nature of this conception of the people. They tend to sectionalize social life and to entrust each of its sectors to specialists: economists, engineers, political scientists, and so on. If Christianity does not consist in reactivating biblical language by giving back his voice to the common man, the ordinary poor man who is the bearer of a message of freedom, it loses its consistency. Either it vitalizes movements of the poor which judge and check the experts, or it is emptied of all content.

In the same way, those themes relating to material goods, to money, poverty, riches, accumulation, preoccupation, and so on, the themes of the Sermon on the Mount, cannot be reduced to mere intentions or to inward dispositions. They define a mode of relationship between men and nature. They are the principles of a civilization in which man's relations with things are not the source of human conflicts but the basis of an existence with others. Incompatibility between the service of God and the service

of money is a principle which puts in question the fundamental
structures of a civilization. Interpreting the Bible consists in
extracting from its themes that light which enlightens the bases
of the civilization of our time. It is no longer possible to reduce
the Sermon on the Mount to a programme of asceticism for a
few experts: it has to do with a word addressed to the whole of
mankind—one as valid for economists, engineers and planners
as for all responsible men.

That's the context in which we ought to read what Paul says
explicitly about freedom. The space available here isn't enough
for a detailed discussion of the doctrine of freedom from sin, the
law and death or the "principles" or "powers" of this world.
But I can remind you that the Pauline freedom is not the inward
freedom of detachment from all material life. It is not the empty
availability of the man who is no longer linked to anything, as
in eastern spirituality.

That man is free who lives under the movement of the Spirit
and produces fruits of the Spirit. To be free is to be with others,
to enter into new human relations inspired by love. The actual
content of freedom is the relation of reciprocal openness and
mutual service between men. There is no such thing as a freedom of man on his own. From the time of the Renaissance
modern western civilization has developed an ideal of individual
liberation consisting of the self-affirmation of the isolated and
autonomous individual: the freedom of the "conquistador." But
to dominate is not to be free; it is to be related by the passion
for domination and to be incapable of love, that is of being a
man. There is liberation only in a new way of communal life
which is also a new relationship between men and nature. Sin is
the rejection of the covenant and the pursuit of salvation in
itself. The law is the pursuit of freedom by means of domination.
Death is the state of man given up to himself, but life is in the
people reunited in Jesus Christ. The powers of this world falsely
claim to save man without freeing him, and rely on his fear.

Freedom proceeds from the Spirit extended to all men in order
to give birth to a new man, and the Spirit produces a social man,
a man who is mutual service, a man who is public or political,
who lives in full reciprocity. It is the distinction between the
private and the public, the individual and the collective which

is contained in the new covenant. Exegesis cannot consist in a dissolution of this message on the pretext that the social problems of our time are now so complex at this point that only experts have the right to tackle them.

The Johannine doctrine of liberation reveals the same message. It is located in Jesus' controversy with the Jews (chapter 8). The Jews think that they're free but in reality they're slaves. They have turned God's word into a system in which they're imprisoned. They wanted to make it a possession and now they're shut up in their property. They have not only sworn fealty to death, but they belong to it in such a way that death has become the instrument by which they believe they will be able to save themselves. They have become the slaves of death. They will feel forced to kill Jesus in order to save themselves. They have seen that Jesus was a threat to their closed system. They didn't want to open up to the rest of the world and lose their privilege. Liberation consists in opening up to the Spirit and to a universal love in Jesus, by him and as him. There is freedom only in the acceptance of the unity of chapter 17. There is life only in this new way of "being with".

In short, liberation is the coming of that nation in which there are no more masters and slaves, men and women, intellectuals and illiterates, rich and poor, but where relations between man and nature are no longer the closed field of fratricidal struggles, and men no longer manufacture the arms which will allow them to dominate their own kind. How can this news of the kingdom of God enlighten today's world? That is the problem of the present-day Church, and therefore of its theology. The Church does not exist for itself, but in order to make this light actual for this world.

III. Aspects of Liberation

The dominant nations today tend to submit to "technologists". Their "techniques" assure them many advantages and they fear that any questioning of plans drawn up by experts will have unfavourable consequences for their material progress. Blackmail by experts is paralysing the Churches. Christians feel devoid of arguments that would enable them to question the bases of a civilization which seems to be proceeding all on its own —and all the more effectively the less men intervene in it. There may be a general sickness of civilization, but institutions do not dare to intervene. Men accept their fate as the instruments of civilization and ask only vaguely where it is leading them. Christians suspect that it is leading them astray from the concerns of the Gospel. It is difficult for a rich man to get away from his riches so that he can really grasp the problem of life; he is a prisoner of his possessions. Basic political problems are left to the experts—those who (precisely because of their expertise) are not liable to perceive them: economists, military men, policemen....

It is in the nations of the Third World that the simple and basic questions are posed: there they are lived out in all their urgency; there the poor have no property to defend. There the sickness of present-day civilization appears obvious, for there is no way to hide it; and there the experts reveal their limitations. Hence the attempts at a "theology of liberation".

Theologies of liberation are not arrived at without difficulty. They are subject to various illusions. First and foremost among these is a flight into the past: the easiest way to think of liberation is as a straightforward rejection of all the structures of, and all connections with, the dominant civilization. The result would be autonomy, but in the midst of a pre-technical age. A very old illusion of poor Christians is to have recourse to more "human" though archaic structures than those of a modernized world where the techniques favour much stronger relations of domination.

The other illusion is a flight into the future: that is, into utopia. But the Christian function is not to feed utopias which the shock of reality must sooner or later give the lie to. In Latin America a number of Christian movements have experienced this temptation towards a utopia (Brazil, Chile, for example) and the awakenings have been harsh ones.

Christianity will take on a messianic attraction when, in the poor countries, it turns to social life. The biblical concerns arouse a hope of immediate realization. Ignorance of real political life and real history makes the Kingdom of God seem to appear on the horizon of an immediate future: there is a fervent entry into "history" as if there were a praxis at the end of which "liberation" might be found. In Latin America even Marxism is lived as a messianism. *A fortiori* political movements depend on Christian inspiration. The themes of exodus and the messianic prophecies seem to announce the arrival of a new people, and that people is the oppressed world delivered from its chains. Messianism is as old as the Bible itself. Among the poor and the oppressed Bible reading has always been messianic. Why should it be any different nowadays? Wasn't Jesus himself understood in a messianic sense? The problem of the theology of liberation is precisely one of passing from the stage of messianism (the ideology of the spontaneous practice of Christian movements) to Christianity (that is, to historical realism, and to the "mystery" of the kingdom of God).

When they enter on to the path of politics, the Third-World countries find themselves directly faced with a dilemma which is eminently that of all Christian movements—nationalism or revolution. The ideologies of the Third World seem to have as their mission the overcoming of the dilemma by manufacturing systems of ideas which can be grouped under the heading "national revolution". But in reality any claim to homogeneity on the part of such ideologies collapses. In fact the constant dilemma is whether to look for freedom by way of national sovereignty, national power, and an imitation of western society by using the same means as western society (and how is this assimilation of the western model to be avoided if a nation is to control its own destiny). Since western society is the work of a middle class in control of expertise, national freedom tends to be bought by means of the formation and development of a national bourgeoisie (possibly under the guise of a popular or socialist ideology, a supreme ruse of history). Another dilemma is how to look for a new societal model, while rejecting entirely or in part the instruments of power of modern society, and while running the risk of staying on the periphery of world history. How, in short, is one to know if a new societal model constitutes a prophecy of the future or a place on the periphery of evolution?

The present debates in Marxism show that no ideology can claim to have overcome the problem. National power is a condition for a nation about to master its own destiny. But it binds it to the technical necessities of its construction. It delivers it (much weaker than the older nations) to the ambitions and to the domination of the new middle classes (civil but above all military). Freedom is the search for a new way of communal life and for a subordination of techniques to a new model of social relations, but how is one to master these techniques if their structure and operation are controlled by centres in the dominant countries?

The same dilemma arises at all levels of social life. It arises at the level of the production of material goods or of labour. Production techniques are neither morally innocent nor socially indifferent. Each system tends to introduce and to maintain this or that type of social relations, this or that type of dependence or domination. The disillusionment of the socialist experiments have shown that there is no level of technical development which necessarily brings with it human relations of freedom. In order to safeguard or to obtain a certain freedom, we have to face up to expertise and economics, and refuse to allow them autonomy to choose and direct. There will be freedom only in this action to control the practice of techniques.

On the level of human action on men, there is the dilemma of politics in the strict sense: the exercise of power. Here too the socialist experiment has shown that there is no such thing as innocent power. All power tends to domination by virtue of its dynamism as soon as it is left to itself. There is no social change without the intervention of political power, but a socialism built by the power of the State, whatever it may be called, is always a system of domination. There is freedom only in the control and limitation of power by the citizens and by private associations. The proletarian State is a myth which serves to conceal the ascent of a new middle class and a new capitalism, as is shown by the development of those countries of eastern Europe which are directed more and more towards the discovery of the merits of capitalism.

Any culture, that is, any system of language and human communication, lends itself to the reinforcement of the structures of economic or political domination. That becomes all the more obvious in the Third World. There is no form of language and no means of communication which does not need to be judged, orientated and disciplined, if we want to prevent the means itself being the culture and subordinating men to its technical necessities.

To the extent that liberation is entrusted to those who know, to the experts, it masks domination. There is no longer a global practice of liberation which could give rise to a science or a global theory. There is a human responsibility, a permanent confrontation between ends and means—ends borne by men; men of pure countenance to whom the Kingdom of God is promised on the one hand, and, on the other, all sciences and techniques. That is why the message of Jesus Christ who is the voice of men (simply as men) is more vital and up to date than ever. It is so above all in dominated and oppressed countries whose mission is irreplaceable but whose paths are sown with traps.

Juan Luis Segundo

Capitalism—Socialism:
A Theological Crux

LATIN American theology, especially the theology of liberation, is reputed to be enthusiastic, ephemeral and rather light-weight in European theological circles, which are used to work of a more developed character. This is naturally of some concern to us, not only because it calls us and our work into question, but because, with rare exceptions, Latin American seminarists continue to be academically formed by a theology which at its best is a copy of the most reputable and up-to-date European theology.

In the formation of the future priests and pastors in Latin America, the theme of liberation frequently appears in a light that is more political and kerygmatic than, properly speaking, theological. On the other hand, it is a fact that the pastoral praxis has been especially responsible for orientating theological thought towards liberation and related themes. Hence the theology of liberation, whatever one's view of the validity of this term, is a spoken much more than a written theology.

It will have been repeatedly made clear in this issue of *Concilium* that the phrase "theology of liberation" does not designate one sector of theology (such as the "theology of work" or the "theology of death"), but the whole of theology itself. It is theology seen not from one of the various possible standpoints, but from the one standpoint indicated by Christian sources as the authentic, privileged one for the right understanding of divine revelation in Jesus Christ.[1]

---

[1] Cf. Gustavo Gutiérrez, *A Theology of Liberation* (Orbis Books, Maryknoll, N.Y. 1973) *passim*. This book, and that of Hugo Assmann,

Because of all these factors, I believe that the polemics about the seriousness of the theology of liberation cannot make any advance, except through a concrete problem taken as a test. I prefer to invite the reader to accompany me in a concrete theological experience and put to theology one of the most acute human problems of my Latin American continent—the option between capitalist and socialist society.

Before beginning, I ask the reader to keep in mind one decisive datum. This option, in our case, is not made in relation to the possibilities offered by a developed capitalism or socialism. The choice we have to make is not between society as it exists in the USA or society as it exists in the Soviet Union. Our option is taken from the oppressed periphery of the great economic empires. What socio-political scheme can be chosen now from our own underdeveloped condition, which will at the same time be effective and coherent with the kind of society which we desire for Latin Americans as we know them?

This is the question we put to theology, because it is vital for us. But another question arises immediately. Is it meaningful to put such questions precisely to theology? This is not an easy question to answer.

I will not linger on the classical theological opinion, especially in Catholic circles, which would certainly be in the affirmative, though on the basis of theological assumptions which are very questionable and ultimately, to my mind, unacceptable. In the first place, the question is regarded as suitable because the option belongs to the ambit of moral theology, which has its own procedures. In the second place, it is generally added that the option for socialism is morally unacceptable, because socialism does not recognize the natural right of the human being to private ownership, even of the means of production. Neither the abysmal separation between a dogmatic theology and a moral theology, nor the notion of "natural law", nor especially its application to the defence of the private possession of such means by some people,

<hr>

Opresión-Liberación. Desafío a los cristianos (Montevideo, 1971) are as far as I know the only two books of the theology of liberation which raise the debate to the level of a well-documented scientific dialogue with European theology.

and only some, appear to me to be principles of enough substance to merit particular attention.[2]

The two negative replies appear to me to be more subtle, profound and worthy of attention. These deny the right to put, or
the suitability of putting the capitalist-socialist option to theology. One of these negative replies is of pragmatic origin and
carries more weight in Latin America, while the other is of
theoretical origin and counts for more in Europe

I

The pragmatic negative to any consideration of our problem
follows, as may be imagined, from the task which the Christian
Churches attribute to themselves. As it is a pragmatic negative, it
is particularly interesting for what it does not say, for its hidden
reasons and motives, that is to say, for the theory which under-
lies it.

The refusal to decide one way or another in the problem under
discussion is well exemplified in the answer given by the Catholic
bishops of Chile to this vital question for that country. They
said, "The Church opts for the risen Jesus. . . . The Church makes
no political option—it belongs to all the people of Chile."

What is the logical assumption behind this practical reply?
That it would be senseless to make an absolute value (religious,
pertaining to salvation) depend on a relative value (the preference for one system—always imperfect—of political life).

In intellectual circles, the reactions against this kind of pastoral
practice and its theological implications can reach the point of
contempt. It is none the less true that the great majority of
Christian Churches continue to be officially structured as autonomous centres of salvation. They sincerely believe in this. If
they adopt progressive positions in historical matters, they do so
to the absolute value of salvation which they aim to make their
faithful share in even more attractive. Would it not be possible
and evangelical to invert this order of values and to declare, with
the gospel itself, that the sabbath is made for man and not man
for the sabbath? Could this statement not be given the only

[2] Cf. Juan L. Segundo, *De la sociedad a la teología* (Buenos Aires, 1970),
III, p. 127 ff.

possible translation, namely that human life in society, liberated as far as possible from alienations, constitutes the absolute value, and that all religious institutions, all dogmas, all the sacraments, and all the ecclesiastical authorities, have only a relative, that is, a functional value?

Once more, in Christian milieux capable of theoretical reflection, this inversion of values in accordance with the gospel is relatively easy and is operating in Latin America. But with what result? With this result—that the divergence, antipathy and separation grow deeper all the time between such Christians and the official churches which continue to be structured according to opposing principles.

To return to the point at issue, as long as the Church continues to attribute an absolute value to those objects, words, gestures and authorities which appear to form a vertical link between their faithful and God, and a purely relative value to the historical functionalism of all this, it is not possible to put to theology any question about how to orientate the option of Christians between capitalism and socialism.

We could, as I was saying, leave this question at this point and let pastoral action shoulder the task of explaining to the hierarchy of Christian Churches what the authentic scale of values must be. Perhaps then they would see the need to commit pastoral action to a human problem of the fundamental nature of the one which we are considering. But it is more and more urgent in Latin America, with this pragmatic objection still in view, to draw up as effective a theoretical criticism as possible of these mistaken pastoral motivations.

For this, we could follow the course of European theology and draw on the arsenal of tradition to show from the past how the authentic attitude of the Church towards similar problems was a distinct one in former times. We could trace the point in time when deviation set in, with increasing neglect of the functional role of the whole apparatus of the Church in relation to human history. This would be the road back to the sources, the road followed by Hans Küng, for example, in his works *Infallible?* and *The Structures of the Church*.

In my view, however, there is a very marked tendency in Latin America to approach this kind of pragmatic Church problem by another way, namely through present-day explanations founded on the psycho-social sciences.

What might be, for instance, the psycho-sociological motives for the kind of pragmatic attitudes generally found in the Church today? Latin American theology is orientated towards inter-disciplinary work in this field, through the human sciences. I be-lieve that with their help it is possible for theology to verify the following hypothesis on these same attitudes in the Church. Gestures, formulae, rites and authorities directly related to sal-vation, to the absolute, and so located outside the system of finali-ties within which everything else moves, generally give indication that those who employ them know that if they were introduced into that system they would lose not only their absolute but also their relative value. That is the danger of the absolute—either it is absolute or it is nothing. When the Churches set up as abso-lutes things which they are not, they seek in reality to keep a relative value for them by binding them to human insecurity. As Thorsten Veblen writes in his *Theory of the Leisured Class*:

"Only individuals of unusual temperament can in the long run keep their self-esteem when faced with the contempt of their fellow human beings. There are apparent exceptions to the rule, especially among people of strong religious convictions. But these apparent exceptions are seldom so in reality, since they rely on the supposed approval of some supernatural witness to their acts."[3]

From statements like Veblen's, many scientists will no doubt tend to draw arguments against Christianity in general. Our aim on the contrary is to work across the disciplines with these sci-ences and *make* theology in the real sense of that phrase; this involves retracing the intimate and often unconscious mechan-isms by which we think about God, his message, his Church. We believe that in the field of these inner motivating forces (which are not only theological) are found today at the inter-confessional Christian level, the profound, exciting divergences which, in other ages and with different intellectual instruments, were called Trinitarian or christological controversies.

Is it not in fact a form of heterodoxy to invert the evangelical order of values as it is now being inverted? If the interdisciplin-

[3] Thorsten Veblen, *Theory of the Leisure Class* (New York, 1899).

ary hypothesis is verified, it will also be verified that the hetero-praxis of absolutized Churches rests on a radical heterodoxy—the progressive loss of faith in the gospel of Jesus Christ. Or, to put it another way, the loss of faith in its human functionality.[4]

The task of theology here is to classify the unsuccessful evangelical experiences which are at the base of this ecclesiastical insecurity. Another task is to establish the criteria of an authentic historical functionality of the gospel, as well as its limits, since every incarnation has limits. This leads us once more to the conviction that if the conclusion were reached that the gospel has nothing to say on a human problem so decisive as the alternative between capitalism and socialism, it is clear that it can only have an absolute, not a functional, value, that is to say, no value at all.

II

But apart from the pragmatic objection which has just been rapidly examined by way of example, I said that there is a theoretical objection to any contribution by theology to the political alternative we are examining.

What type of theology from those now practised would serve to orientate us in our choice? Doubtless the political theology or theology of revolution, which arose in the ambit of German Catholic and Protestant thought. Believe it or not, however, neither political theology nor the theology of revolution can meet our needs in the face of this most demanding political and revolutionary alternative.

As I said, Latin America wishes to plan and construct her future. Hence this critically important alternative between two systems and their respective logical arguments, both human and social. According to Metz, "... what distinguishes 'Christian eschatology' from the ideologies of the future in the East and the West, is not that it knows more, but that it knows less about that future which mankind is trying to discern, and that it persists in its lack of that knowledge."[5] Metz holds that an eschatological

[4] Cf. Juan L. Segundo, *Pastoral Latinoamericana. Sus motivos ocultos.* (Buenos Aires, 1972), chap. V ff.

[5] J. B. Metz, *L'homme, Anthropocentrique chrétienne* (Paris, 1971), p. III.

theology ought to know less about capitalism and socialism than the theorists of either system.

What is meant by this? That the Church is much more reticent than any political programme. Hence Metz goes on to write that the Church "must institutionalize that eschatological reserve by establishing itself as an instance of critical liberty in the face of social development in order to reject the tendency of the latter to present itself as absolute."[6]

Again we come up against the relative-absolute distinction. And again the concrete political option is considered to be relative. The difference this time is that the absolute here is not the Church but something the Church serves: the eschatological Kingdom of God, the ultimate future, which comes down from God himself to mankind.

Here the Church gives full recognition to its functionality in relation to the eschatological Kingdom. Its own triumph is not what matters to it, but the triumph of the Kingdom. So Moltmann writes: "The universalism of the crucified Christ is realized in the world only through the dialectic of taking sides. The false universalism of the Church (our first, pragmatic objection) is, on the contrary, a premature and inopportune anticipation of the Kingdom of God."[7]

According to these words of Moltmann, the functionality of the Church would consist in preventing "premature and inopportune" anticipations of the Kingdom of God. And he refers expressly to one of them: the false universalism of the Church, that is, the Church absolutized. But in the broader context of his work, it is seen that every historical project has a tendency to the same universalism, the same absolutization. Political theology attacks all kinds of absolutism, whatever their source: whether they come from the past or the future, the East or the West. It de-absolutizes on the same basis the existing order and the order projected.

For this very reason, when many of the writings of the "theology of revolution" are read, the impression is given that the revolution which is there alluded to, resembles the theoretical-

[6] *Ibid.*, p. 136.

[7] J. Moltmann, "Dieu dans la révolution" in *Discussion sur la théologie de la révolution* (Paris, 1972), p. 72.

Cartesian revoluton of methodical doubt, rather than practical revolution. One may say that it revolutionizes our way of viewing politico-social systems from our establishment inside them; but it does not choose between one system and another. If it has any tendency, if it inclines to one side, it will probably be against the order established today; the capitalist order where that prevails, the socialist order where that prevails. More than that, as the two regimes coexist today, the "eschatological" criticisms converge today towards a common relativization, which is revolutionary only in name.

By another, more profoundly theological approach we reach the same conclusion, namely, that it does not do to ask theology about the relationship between the revealed message and the political option between capitalism and socialism. We have already said that this was not to be done, so as not to weigh down the absolute—the Kingdom—with the weight of the relative-transient political systems. And the profound reason is that relative values are not even fragments of the absolute value. They remain definitively within their sphere of relativity.

German political theology chooses with the utmost care the terms which indicate this relationship between a relative political order and the absolute eschatological order: anticipation (Moltmann), analogical image or analogy (Weth) and outline (Metz). All these terms systematically and expressly reject every idea of causality.

But who consecrates his life to an "analogy"? Who dies for an "outline"? Who moves a human mass, a whole people, in the name of an "anticipation"?

There is in Latin America a theological tendency which as we know has taken to calling itself the theology of liberation. Let us overlook the question as to whether the name is well chosen or what divergences may separate theologians who are included in this denomination. There is something common and basic for all of them—the view that men, on a political as well as individual basis, construct the Kingdom of God from within history now.[8] As can be seen, we cannot minimize the radical

---

[8] Cf. Gustavo Gutiérrez, op. cit., p. 212 ff. Cf. also Hugo Assmann Opresión-Liberación. Desafío a los cristianos, op. cit., p. 154 ff. and Conrado Eggers Lan, Cristianismo y nueva ideología (Buenos Aires, 1968), p. 46 ff.

divergence which exists between this approach and the denial of causality (even an imperfect and partial causality) on principle to all political parties in relation to the definitive Kingdom.

The argument advanced by German political theology for this negation is none other than the very basis of the Reformation— the doctrine of Paul on justification by faith alone, and not by works.

One of the participants in the discussion on the theology of revolution, Rudolf Weth, outlines this argument clearly and summarizes it thus: "God himself effects the decisive revolutionary action for the coming of his Kingdom. That action cannot be effected or replaced by any human action."[9] Weth continues by supporting this argument with a decisive text of Luther in which the latter transfers the principle of justification by faith alone on to the plane of the universal Kingdom. Luther comments on the passage of Matthew (25. 34) in which the universal Judge calls the good to possess the Kingdom prepared for them since the beginning. He goes on, "How could (the Sons of the Kingdom) merit what already belongs to them and has been prepared for them since before they were created? It would be more exact to say that it is the Kingdom of God which merits us as possessors.... The Kingdom of God is already prepared. But the children of God must be prepared in view of the Kingdom, so that it is the Kingdom which merits the children, and not the children of God who merit the Kingdom."[10]

It is obvious that this exegesis radically disqualifies any option between any socio-political systems which aim to prepare in a causal manner the Kingdom of God. It will perhaps be said that this is only the sector of political theology that proceeds from the Reformation, but it is a striking fact that Roman Catholic theology in Europe, especially since Vatican II, is drawing nearer to the Lutheran positions on justification. Hence, on the points we are discussing now, no marked differences can be seen between one and the other.

If right and left are broadly identified—as occurs in Latin

[9] R. Weth, "La Théologie de la révolution dans la perspective de la justification et du royaume" in *Discussion sur la théologie de la révolution, op. cit.,* p. 86.
[10] M. Luther, *Œuvres* (Geneva, 1958), V, p. 120 (Quoted by Weth *ibid.*).

American usage—with the capitalist and the socialist option respectively, then we can certainly supply some proof of what has just been said. Let us take, for example, the general comment which a French Catholic theologian, Henri de Lavalette, makes about what he calls the "ambiguity" of German political theology. He writes thus: "What does it achieve? Does it divide the Church still more into right-wing Christians and left-wing Christians? Does it allow the existence in a Church with a centrist majority, of a left-wing current of thought? Or is it capable of making Christians face up to their political divisions and see then vis-à-vis reconciliation in Christ? Paul's statement that in Christ Jesus there is neither man nor woman means that the fact of being a man or woman is not an absolute which separates one from the other, allowing only one or the other to be Christians. In the same way the division between right and left—which is a political division and judgment—does not carry with it the exclusive privilege of a Christian label, and could not be put forward as a judgment of God. The Church is open to men and women and to right and left."[11]

As can be seen from this text of Lavalette, the whole weight of theology as a serious science makes it impossible, either by way of the Church or by way of the eschatological Kingdom, for us to throw light on the practical political option which, in Latin America, is the point at which our deepest, total commitments converge.

Having reached this negative conclusion, which appears unacceptable to me, all that I can do is to say a final word about the possibilities of a theology which will be capable of making a decisive contribution to the equally decisive options of our society. In the course of this, some critical revision of the negative arguments so far presented may emerge.

III

Before studying the possible relationship between theology and the political option for capitalism or socialism, two points have to be clarified.

[11] H. de Lavalette "Ambiguïtés de la théologie politique" in *Recherches de Sciences Religieuses,* Oct.-Dec. 1971 (Vol. 59, No. 4), p. 559.

The first is that by "socialism" we do not mean a complete, long-term social project, endowed with a particular ideology or philosophy. We give the name of socialism to a political regime in which the ownership of the means of production is removed from individuals and handed over to higher institutions whose concern is the common good. By capitalism we understand the political regime in which the ownership of the goods of production is open to economic competition. It may be objected—why not give a more detailed account of the socialist model? Or why not speak of the possibilities of a moderate, renovated capitalism? There is one very simple reason for not doing this—we cannot foresee or control the universe of the future. The only real, possible option remaining to us is within our own countries as they are. Today the only thing we can do is to decide whether we are going to leave to individuals and private groups, or take away from them, the right to possess the means of production which exist in our countries. That is what we call the option for capitalism or socialism.

The second point that we must clarify in advance is that by theology we do not simply mean the scientific investigation of dogmas. By this is meant the study of how they came to be formulated and how, keeping in mind changes in mentality and language, they must be formulated today in order to preserve authentic continuity. As I remarked before, I believe that this scientific discipline, relatively autonomous, the concern of professionals, has for centuries now been channelling much of its content towards a conservative ideological function. This is not so much because it always proposes "conservative" dogmas, but because its very autonomy in relation to the concrete Christian praxis leaves the latter on a secondary plane, open to criteria independent of faith. So there has taken shape, in isolation from dogma, moral theology which, while it is not temporal, is profoundly similar to the civic morality required by established society. And on the other hand, the dogmatic theologian has become simply one among many purveyors of abstract culture which the consumer society accepts and even protects.

By theology we therefore understand in a much more direct fashion *fides quaerens intellectum*, faith in search of its own understanding, to orientate the historical praxis.[12] We do not

[12] Cf. Gustavo Gutierrez, *op. cit.,* all of Chap. I.

accept that a single dogma can be studied under any other final criterion than that of its social impact on the praxis.[13]

Keeping in mind what we understand by socialism and what we understand by a theological task, we can consider the problem of the relationship between them. Of course there is no question of a moral theology being in any way responsible for directing the investigation. Our search is for a positive or negative relationship between dogma and socialism.

But when was dogma ever applied to political events? To begin with, it certainly was in the preaching of the great prophets of Israel. And if I am not mistaken we will see that the thought, or if you like the theology of the prophets, has little to do with current ecclesiological assumptions or with the criteria of European political theology today.[14]

The prophet is not, of course, a seer in the modern sense of possessing ability to see into the future. But he is a seer in the sense that he discovers under the superficial event a will, a plan, an evaluation of God. But if this were all, the seer would become a legislator rather than a prophet. He is a prophet because in some way he projects into the future the historical consequences of that divine design or evaluation of events. With his vision of the divine present, he builds a project for the future which is historic and human.

An example of this kind of project was that put forward by Jeremiah when he announced to all those who were still in Jerusalem after the exile, that it was the will of Yahweh for them to remain there and not emigrate to Egypt. He associated this project so closely with God's will that he predicted to all those who emigrated to Egypt that not one of them would survive. How did the theological thinking of the prophet function? In the first place, a deeper vision than normal showed him God acting in events and judging them according to their true value. The God of Israel, being who he was (theology), could not see with other eyes what was happening. He could not attribute another value to historical facts. Starting from that conviction,

[13] Cf. H. Assmann, *op. cit.*, p. 86 ff.
[14] Cf. Gerhard von Rad, *Old Testament Theology* II (New York, 1965), *passim*.

the prophet imagined a future in accord with the divine evaluation, and gave it a corresponding certainty. It was a "political"
project, but the prophet did not "eschatologize" it. He did not
leave his hearers feeling equally critical about the historical
option, which is relative, and the Kingdom of God, which is
absolute.

His prophecy, considered as a vision of the future, was even
disproved by events. Respecting this political fallibility of the
prophets, Henri Cazelles writes in his work on the Bible and
politics: "A strange fact must be singled out in the political
activity of the prophets—as a general rule it ended in political
failure. But despite that failure, the disciples of the prophets
collected together their oracles and recognized their validity as the
word of God."[15] We can only add that as it was then, so it will
always be where a prophetic theology is being exercised.

Every theology which refuses to make a theological judgment,
that is, to invoke the word of God, about a political reality, on
the pretext that science cannot demonstrate that the future will
beyond doubt be better, draws further away from the prophetic
function.

The classical prophetic stage of the Old Testament can be
reproached, with some reason, for having a vision of the Kingdom of God which was not eschatological or at least very rudi-
mentary in that respect. Eschatology is much more evident after
the exile and restoration.

I, therefore, think it important to by-pass a few stages and come
to the New Testament polemics between Jesus and the theology
of his period, as the synoptics present it to us. I believe that very
little attention has been paid to the major fact of the polemics,
namely that the radical difference between one camp and the
other does not lie in the theological content under debate. At
least, it is due very much less to this than to a disagreement
about the way to make theology and about the instruments used
by one camp or the other in the theological task.

We will now consider this difference. For the moment we will
put aside the current debate on the indifference or commitment

[15] Henri Cazelles, "Bible et politique" in *Recherches de Sciences Religieuses*, Oct.-Dec. 1971 (Vol. 59, No. 4), p. 512.

of Jesus regarding politics as such. I may, however, be permitted one comment on this subject before going on. My view is that in the various attempts to show that Jesus displayed some interest in politics and in political liberation, there is an anachronistic reliance on the few data afforded by the synoptics about the relations of Jesus with the Roman Empire. For many exegetes, this constitutes the political structure of the time. To classify the political attitude of Jesus it is recalled that he had zealot (that is, seditious) disciples, that he was condemned to death as subversive of the Empire, etc.

The anachronism in all this, if I am not mistaken, consists in localizing the "political element" of the period of Jesus in the structures of the Roman Empire because they are what most resemble a modern political empire. The fact is overlooked that, at that time, the political life, the civic organization of the Jewish multitudes, their burdens, their oppression, their differing social and cultural situation, depended much less on the Roman Empire and much more on the theology ruling in the groups of scribes and pharisees. They, and not the Empire, imposed intolerable burdens on the weak and dispensed themselves from them, so establishing the true socio-political structure of Israel. To that extent, the counter-theology of Jesus was much more political than pronouncements or acts against the Roman Empire would have been.

To return, however, to the question of the confrontation of these two theologies, it should be noted that they have in common the attempt to find the divine presence and orientation in the historical events that were happening.

The theology opposed to Jesus is described in the synoptics as seeking in history for "signs from heaven" or better, "signs proceeding from heaven." With the help of the immediate context (and remembering the signs from heaven that Satan suggests to Jesus in the desert), we can characterize these signs from heaven as anticipations, outlines, analogies of a strictly divine action, something which by its very nature cannot be attributed to man or, still less, to the devil. How else can an historical happening be designated as a sign proceeding from heaven?

What are the signs opposed by Jesus to these signs from heaven? What he calls the "signs of the times": concrete transformations effected by him in the historical present, and entrusted by him to his disciples for then and for the future. It will be remembered that, to the eschatological question of the disciples of the Baptist about "he who is to come", Jesus replies with signs that are historical, relative, extremely ambiguous, at a vast distance from the absolute and definitive. The deaf hear, but what? The lame walk, but where? The sick are cured, but will they not perhaps succumb to new and more decisive illnesses? The dead rise again, but is it worth while if, after their pain and anguish, they have to yield again to death in the future? The poor receive the good news, but when will their real condition change, and who will change it?

However, here begins the different understanding of the signs, which is at the basis of the two theologies. The woman who requires signs from heaven is concerned to know whether the events, the same events which Jesus alluded to, were beyond all doubt from God, or if they could proceed from Satan. On the basis of his theology of the signs, Jesus replies with a boldness which scientific Christian theology has completely lost. He says practically the following: "The sign is in itself so clear that even if it is Satan who liberates these men from their ills, it is because the Kingdom of God has arrived and is among you." With this remark he discounts totally any theological criterion applied to history, which is not the direct and present evaluation of the event.

But it is evident that for this judgment of the event in itself, from the point of view of its human value, theology has need of an instrument of cognition which is likewise being minimized or simply neglected by scientific theology. We could call it, in modern terms, historical sensibility. In the synoptics, the decisive term constantly being employed is that of "heart": a hard, closed heart or a sensitive, open heart.

In a theological dispute concerning what was a commandment of God and what was purely human tradition, Jesus paradoxically places the commandments of God on the side of spontaneity of heart open to others, and purely human traditions on the side of reason calculating with the heart closed. In fact an event cannot be judged in itself if it does not respond to the expectation of a sensitive heart. Reason will remain paralysed be-

fore its ambiguity, and the arguments drawn from it will be no
more than the servants of egoism.

It can be understood how in the evangelical polemics about
the unpardonable sin, in the context of the cure of the dumb
man, Jesus declares that it does not consist in theological judgment on the origin of his work—divine or satanic. Blasphemy
arising from a mistaken line of argument is always pardonable.
The unpardonable sin is not to recognize as liberation what truly
is liberation and to use theology in order to render the liberation
of a man something odious. The sin against the Spirit is not to
recognize with "theological" joy a concrete liberation happening
before one's eyes.

I say liberation because Luke, who is the only evangelist to
describe the context of the cure, is also the only one to add a
decisive trait to the parable in which Jesus describes the cosmic
dimension of his work, the only theological sign that can precede
the recognition of his person. With Jesus, the "strong man" who
dominated and enslaved mankind is conquered and disarmed.
According to Luke, the spoils of the struggle do not pass to a
new master: they are distributed to their natural recipients; such
as speech to the dumb man.

To end this series of characteristics of the theology of Jesus,
it is important to indicate how he calls the specific instances of
liberation which he effects. We have already said that the reason
here comes up against ambiguous features, especially if the future
is looked to. Despite this, Jesus gives these instances the most
absolute name in the theology of the time: salvation. Far from
de-absolutizing, we can say that he absolutizes imprudently.
Just as he called cures of uncertain consequence the "arrival of
the Kingdom", so he calls a momentary, ambiguous, still unrealized decision of Zacchaeus "the entry into salvation". "Your
faith has saved you", he said on more than one occasion to people
who obtained favours or cures (always uncertain and transient)
from him.

What is the source of the invincible repugnance of modern
scientific theology, especially European theology, to pronounce
on political alternatives exactly parallel to the alternatives that
were the object of the theology of Jesus throughout his preaching?

When the political theologian of Europe requires Latin

Americans to put forward a project for a socialist society which will guarantee in advance that the evident defects of known socialist systems will be avoided, why do we not demand of Christ also that before telling a sick man who has been cured "your faith has saved you", he should give a guarantee that that cure will not be followed by even graver illnesses.

Historical sensibility to hunger and illiteracy, for example, calls for a society where competition and profit will not be the law and where the provision of basic food and culture to an underdeveloped people will be regarded as a liberation.

In relation to future problems, this may seem of lesser importance in well-off countries. But, among us, it is plain for all to see. We live with it twenty-four hours a day. What scientific demands will prevent theology from saying, when these evils are eliminated, "your faith has saved you"? It all consists in giving theological status to an historical event in its absolute elemental simplicity: "Is it lawful on a sabbath day to do good instead of evil, to save a life instead of destroying it?"

All that has been said in the last part may seem evangelical preaching rather than a serious study of theological methodology. It is quite certain that theological methodology has long looked for its criteria in the analogy with other sciences and not in evangelical preaching. It prefers the categories and certainties of other human sciences to the apparent simplicity of the thought of Jesus, and of the primitive Church. I believe that it is necessary to translate into modern methodological terms the original demands of a theological task which will truly be an understanding of the faith confronting history.

1. The eschatological aspect of all Christian theology, far from relativizing the present, binds it to the absolute. Any effective human mobilization of resources requires this absolute relationship, but it can degenerate and this is what the eschatological element forestalls—a degeneration into inhuman rigidity or stagnation or a tendency to sacralize the existing order merely because it is there.

2. It follows that the eschatological element in Christian theology does not define its *content* vis-à-vis secular ideologies, or the function of the ecclesial community in the midst of the society around it, which is the view European political theology appears

to take, either implicitly or explicitly. Eschatology affects only the *form* of theology, the way it accepts absolute commitments. The stress given to eschatological influence depends on a just evaluation, always under reassessment, of the *kairos,* that is, the liberating opportunity. The critical operation that follows from eschatology is not rectilinear but dialectic.

3. To make the Lutheran rediscovery of personal justification by faith without works the key to all biblical exegesis is quite indefensible, particularly in cosmology and ecclesiology. In other words, it is impossible to go logically from the Pauline insistence on avoiding a paralysing concern with justification of self, to the communal demands of the building of the Kingdom. The whole of Scripture is thrown off balance. What is built up in the cosmos effectively and definitively by the disinterested love of men? What does that practical violence consist of, which tears the Kingdom away from utopia and places it squarely among men? These major biblical questions have no meaning if one begins from an *a priori* position that the Kingdom is already built in all its perfection, and only awaits the entry into it of every man by faith.

4. Christian theology will have to be based much more on a sensitive appreciation of what liberates man here and now. This is opposed to the type of science which hopes to foresee and exclude now all the errors and dangers of the future by means of an adequate model, or which claims to criticize and relativize every historical step forward which cannot guarantee these safeguards. Theology has set out to be the science of the unchangeable, in the midst of the fluctuations of human life. It must become once more, like the theology of the Gospel itself, the theology of *fidelity,* which is based on the Unchangeable, and guides the adventure of history through all the adjustments imposed by facts.

5. Consequently, theology does not find on the eschatological horizon any possibility of flying along a middle course equally above the political right and left. The right and the left are not simply two sources of social projects which are subjected to the judgment of a centrally-situated reason. As Martin Lotz observed, the objective of left-wing radicalism is the permanent opening up of society to its future. In the sixteenth edition of the Brockhaus encyclopaedia, the following definition of the left appears:

"the conquest of that which is still without form, of that which is still unrealized, of that which is still in a state of utopia."[16] For that very reason the sensibility of the left is an intrinsic feature of an authentic theology. It must be the necessary form of a reflection whose key quality is historical sensibility.

6. The relationship with a liberating event, no matter how ambiguous and provisional (as in the examples from the gospel), derives, from the strength of God himself who promotes it, a genuinely causal character with respect to the definitive Kingdom of God. This causality is partial, fragile, often erroneous and having to be remade, but it is something very different from anticipations, outlines or analogies of the Kingdom. In the face of options between racial separation and full community of rights, free international demand and supply and a balanced market (with an eye to the underprivileged countries) or capitalism and socialism, what is at stake is no mere analogy of the Kingdom. What is at stake, in a fragmentary fashion if you like, is the eschatological Kingdom itself, whose realization and revelation are awaited with anguish by the whole universe.

In my view, finally, the work of theology in Latin America is moving in the direction which I have just outlined. I am aware that a careful scrutiny of the lines of argument suggested here will lead to the conclusion that I have delivered a radical criticism of European theology, even the most progressive. I am not denying this, though exceptions do exist. It seems to me that theology in the course of the centuries followed its own paths and, like the Church itself often enough, did not allow itself to be judged by the word of God. To get closer to that word, and to the way it becomes human thought committed to history, seems to many of us in Latin America a motive for great hope.

Translated by J. P. Donnelly

[16] Martin Lotz, "Le concept de révolution dans la discussion œcuménique" in *Discussion sur la théologie de libération, op. cit.*, p. 32. In the same sense, and although the word "left" is absent, the following remarks are relevant: "A solidarity of faith unites Christians with the stranger who is always unknown also ... Christians have always had a privileged place for the prisoner, the refugee, the poor and the foreigner"; see M. de Certeau, *L'Étranger ou l'union dans la différence* (Paris, 1969) pp. 12-13. It is plain enough who (between left and right) shows continuing signs of this feeling of solidarity.

PART II
BULLETINS

Raúl Vidales

Some Recent Publications in Latin America on the Theology of Liberation

TO GIVE a chronological account of the theological movement of liberation is not an easy task. Its origin and evolution have been complex and as yet there is no critical study that is sufficiently thorough for it to be used as a reliable guide.

The impact of a new historical experience on the consciousness of some Christian groups in Latin America has led to theological reflection, which has gradually assumed clearer outlines. The crisis of development is generally regarded as the turning-point towards liberation. In this convergence on change, from the socio-economic, political, cultural, ethnic and religious standpoints, the active presence of committed Christians has become a new factor in the move to discover the original Latin American historical vocation. The process of theological reflection on liberation has become more and more explicitly formulated since the year 1965.

It was the CELAM meeting at Medellín (1968) which marked a decisive moment in the development of the theology of liberation. Although it is not quite true to say it was born on that occasion, the future theological movement and its task received both official welcome and the impulse to move forward in the perspective of liberation.[1]

[1] On the occasion of the fifth anniversary of this meeting there have been study conferences which have concentrated on the theological dimension. "Seminario de Teología Latinoamericana" (Bogotá, August 31 – October 31, 1973). "Medellín—cinco años después—sigue el desafío", Cuadernos de estudio No. 5, I.S.A.L. (August 1973, Santiago de Chile).

Many Christians felt that they were being interpreted at Medellín. Now, five years after this event, it continues to stand as a challenge to commitment and reflection. The movement of liberation, which had grown in strength in the years preceding Medellín, is drawn together, and beyond the texts themselves it endures as a movement and an inspiration for Christians, with its exhortation and stimulus, enabling them to be less sluggish, complacent and set in their ways. Since Medellín, theological reflection and writing on liberation have not only become explicit but have also become more intensive.[2]

I. The Acquisitions

Speaking in retrospect and with reference to the publications of greatest relevance and weight, the term "acquisitions" can legitimately be used of the theology of liberation and of the advances made in the new spiritual experience of committed Christians.[3]

A certain consensus can now be discerned, which has been defined as the *loci theologici* of the theology of liberation. It could be said that we are facing a restless theology which is constructed in the course of human experience. This means that its themes and questions are elaborated on the basis of life itself and in essential confrontation with the Word of God. Theology means therefore expressing the "second word" on the basis of lived faith.

To speak of the theology of liberation is to face up to the old problem of the relationship between faith and human existence, but now within the framework of "oppression-liberation". What

[2] E. Pironio, "Teología de la Liberación, in *Teología-PUC* 8 (Buenos Aires, 1970), pp. 7–28; "Teología de la Liberación", I and II, in *Criterio*, 43 (1607–8) (Buenos Aires 1970), pp. 783–9, 822–24; G. Gutiérrez, *Líneas pastorales de la Iglesia en América Latina* (Montevideo, 1968); *Hacia una teología de la Liberación* (Montevideo, 1969); *A Theology of Liberation* (Maryknoll, N.Y. 1973); "Evangelio y praxis de liberación" in *Fe cristiana y cambio social en América Latina* (Salamanca, 1973); H. Assmann, *Opresión-Liberación, desafío a los cristianos* (Montevideo, 1971); E. Dussel, *Caminos de liberación latinoamericana* (Buenos Aires, 1972); S. Galilea, *Contemplación y apostolado* (Bogotá, 1973).

[3] S. Galilea, "¿A los pobres se les anuncia el evangelio?" in *Colecc. IPLA*, 11 (Bogotá, 1972), pp. 37–41.

relationship is there between salvation and the historical process of liberation? In this task, theology makes no *a priori* diagnosis, but looks in the first instance to the answer of concrete faith.

"The option for the poor," Gustavo Gutiérrez has said, "for the exploited classes and for the struggles of the Latin American proletariat, the perception of political affairs as a dimension requiring scientific thinking over the whole range of human existence (and with the resultant inevitable conflicts), the discovery of evangelical poverty as offering solidarity with the poor and a protest against their poverty—all this has led us to a different way of understanding ourselves as men and Christians."[4]

This option involves a concrete response of faith and is the major fact and the *locus theologicus*. Also, this new spiritual experience indicates a new historical context of living as the place of encounter with God, and therefore inaugurates a new understanding of faith.[5] In this view, historical reflection is not formulated as an ideology justifying positions already taken up, but as a critical thinking of experimental faith, giving a reason for hope from within the heart of political commitment itself. In this way, the critical function of theology keeps the Christian permanently disestablished and, while urging him to commit himself to liberation, maintains him in a situation and attitude from which he can relativize systems. He will not fall into the temptation of absolutizing historical models, for he knows that no one of them is adequate for the building up of the Kingdom of God. In this context, faith appears to us more and more as a liberating praxis. The committed Christian rediscovers the new world of the other, that is of his neighbour, seen with emphasis on his relationships as a citizen, and existing as a social class dominated by the exploiting classes and in an antagonistic relationship to them.[6] In a global political situation, and with the growing process of political consciousness, Christian faith necessarily involves a political dimension, not as something added, but as the very essence of the act of faith lived out in its concrete framework of historical praxis.[7]

[4] G. Gutiérrez, "Fe cristiana y praxis de liberación", in *Signos de Liberación* (Lima, 1973).

[5] *Ibid*.

[6] *Ibid*.

[7] H. Assmann, *op. cit.*, pp. 20 *et seq.*

From this specific context theology builds itself up as "a critical reflection from and about the historical praxis in confrontation with the Word of God lived and accepted in faith, a faith
which reaches us across multiple—and at times ambiguous—
historical mediations".[8] The theology of liberation is constituted
in this way as a committed service to Christians who have accepted the challenge of living the faith within socio-cultural categories which differ from and conflict with one another. This
theological task, rather than being a new theology, perhaps
widens the horizon towards a new manner of theologizing.[9] The
novelty of the other and his world are only discovered by faith,
beyond our sphere of understanding and the ability to re-discover
the new meaning of daily living as it reveals itself from our
understanding of the faith means that the road the people follow
towards liberation can be thought out in a Christian way. The
capacity to discern the Christian fact underlying every historical
event and to have the nerve to proclaim it, means that prophecy
has been restored as a daily constituent of faith. In this way, the
theology of liberation becomes "a theology of salvation in the
concrete historical and political conditions of today."[10] This theological perspective can, moreover, only operate within a single
vision of history, in which it develops (as a theology which is
aware of priorities in the challenge it faces) beyond the private,
domestic boundaries of religious living. Hence, for some, when
this theology is identified as "a reflection which starts from the
praxis," it can be said to define itself as a "praxeology".[11]

On the other hand, when the theology of liberation is defined
as a critical reflection starting from the faith as a liberating historical praxis, two consequences follow. It becomes as it were
a second act in relation to the first act of Christian commitment,
and the second word in relation to the first word of the human
sciences, particularly those whose analyses and diagnoses impinge
directly on oppression-liberation. Hence our new understanding
of faith not only introduces the Christian to a world which has
been scientifically elucidated and stands in need of a qualitative

[8] G. Gutiérrez, *op. cit.*
[9] E. Dussel, *op. cit.*, p. 16.
[10] G. Gutiérrez, *op. cit.*
[11] H. Assmann, *op. cit.*, pp. 86–105.

transformation, but in addition opens up for him an historical perspective that is best suited to the free growth of man, and therefore more in consonance with the dynamism of love that operates from faith.

The quest for liberation always basically involves the creation of a new man. But what is the meaning of this struggle, this creation? What is the significance of this option for man, of a new departure in history, of orientation towards the future?[12] Three tasks result from this.

The theology of liberation is concerned with fundamental theological subjects such as creation and salvation, the eschatological promises, Christ the Liberator, institutionalized violence and sin, the Kingdom of God, and so on. This is not done as simple repetition, or by the use of comparison or parallelism, but through the specific, peculiar way in which these realities are believed and lived by Christians convinced that "this is the moment to devise creative imaginative action along the lines required, and especially, to carry it to its conclusion with the boldness of spirit and the equilibrium that come from God."[13]

Thus, the general subject-matter of the theology of liberation is that of all true theology, but the emphasis and the way themes are approached, treated, structured and defined are different. Hence the stress placed on reiterating that this theological task aims to inaugurate a new method of Christian reflection from and about faith as an historical praxis. It is, moveover, identified as a theology of salvation made specific by the particular conditions of the Latin American situation.

II. An Impasse?

At historical moments of essential hostility, when Latin American plans for liberation give the impression of having been completely frustrated, Christians must profoundly reassess their experience and maintain their position in the area of questions and challenges.

At present, equivocation, misunderstanding and ignorance

[12] See G. Gutiérrez, *Theology of Liberation.*
[13] *Documents of the Second General Conference of Latin American Bishops, Medellín, Colombia, Aug.-Sept. 1968* (Bogotá, 1970).

threaten to bring about a difficult situation in the process already set in motion by the acquisitions of the theology of liberation. Advance is difficult in every field and a certain repetitiveness has made itself evident. In some topics it has even become obsessive, in areas of theological work where new conquests and imports are awaited.

The first obstacle is language. A language of liberation is often proclaimed, but a kind of fashionable lexicon can lead to verbal magic, with words becoming mere consumer products. In other cases the same phonetic terms are used, but with different meaning and content. Discussion then runs along different or parallel paths, but makes dialogue between sectors, which, while apparently speaking the same language, are radically divided from each other, quite impossible. More serious is that the language of liberation is often used to express inappropriate meanings, to attribute to the theme of liberation intentions which are not its own or even contradict what it stands for.

The theology of liberation is constantly confronted with the problem of expressing itself intelligibly to those whom it aims to help. This means that we have to take care not to use the language of other disciplines uncritically, so that the original Message is not reduced to cultural statements of a given system.[14] The language of the theology of liberation must not be reduced to a scientific or ideological language. It must beware of the historically empty statements without situational content. It must avoid being absolutist, dogmatic and uniform and must always be open to the historical verification of new, multiform elements of significance. Without losing its political commitment and concrete historical application, it must transmit the Christian Message in its pure state.

The deepest concern of the theology of liberation lies in the passage "from action through the word to the word of action" as a concrete verification.[15] The tendency, even on the part of some sympathizers, to abuse or manipulate the language of liberation makes the double task facing the theology of liberation all the

[14] S. Galilea, *Pastoral y Lenguaje* (Bogota, 1973), pp. 95 ff; J. C. Scannone, "El lenguaje teológico de la liberación", in *Vispera* 30 (Montevideo, 1973), p. 41; H. Assmann, *op. cit.*, p. 37.
[15] H. Assmann, *op. cit.*, p. 42.

more urgent—on the one hand, purification and, on the other, creativity. But, when all is said and done, a committed theology can never avoid the risks incurred by the inevitable mediations of the impure language of cultures, on pain of remaining outside history and becoming irrelevant. Another criticism made of this theology is that it has fallen into the error of socio-political reductionism (faith is political praxis, the salvation of Jesus is socio-economic and political liberation, liberation is revolution, etc.). If theology is reduced in this way, the conclusions of the theological debate become more and more compromising.

If we concentrated our efforts on a really significant elaboration, the above judgments would be seen at once to be erroneous and to indicate considerable ignorance of the interior content of this theology. This is in any case a common problem for any incarnate theology. The word of the Lord and the historical process of liberation—how can theological reflection be structured without either of the two essential poles being sacrificed? The theology of liberation moves within this dialectical tension.

The basic problem is that this theology has always been seen from outside. The price to be paid for being able to understand, criticize and impel it forward is to get inside it. To assimilate it to the theology of revolution would result in attributing to it contents and conclusions which the theology itself would not permit. In Latin America, there has never been any attempt to elaborate a theological theory of revolution. Furthermore, although there is a theological movement with a revolutionary Christian ideology, which is open to the sponsorship of actions and options, the theology of liberation is quite different, in that it starts from the concrete experience of faith committed to the task of historical transformation, but maintains its critical function within this commitment.[16]

There are no grounds for even suspecting that the theology of liberation aims to constitute itself as an ideological or strategic sponsor of a definite political praxis or of a definite school of scientific thought. But of course situations of conflict and front-line themes are, for this theology, the special ingredient of the historical process in which the Christian has to live his faith (institutionalized violence, the class struggle, subversion, politi-

[16] G. Gutiérrez, "Fe cristiana y praxis de liberación", op. cit.

cal options, socialism). The result is that these become themselves *loci theologici.*

III. Tasks

Another characteristic of the present theological reflection on liberation is the explicit recognition that achievements here are not finished themes, but stages in an irreversible process. For that reason, the most urgent task is emphatically regarded not as the repetitive classification of what has already been said, but as the need to deepen and bring to maturity the work begun and creativity in areas where silence and absence still prevail.

Interdisciplinary work is also urgently required. The Latin American perspective on history, anthropology and philosophy, the depth and growing clarity of certain sociological, economic and political themes will certainly contribute much about little-known or untreated aspects of society. The task within the field of theology is still vaster. A new hermeneutic perspective is one of the primary necessities. What is needed is hermeneutics beginning from within the process of theological praxis and reflection, in which any reading of the Bible which fails to take stock of the concrete historical process becomes an illegitimate reading of the Word of the Lord. The Bible must be re-read in the other "bible" of history. The basic text for hermeneutics will be the praxis of faith, the global reality of history clarified by the voice of human sciences and confronting the gospel not as something juxtaposed or only meta-historical, but as the Word sown in the cosmos and in the evolution of human tasks.

No less urgent is the theological task in formulating a new christology and ecclesiology. It is frequently said that committed Christians are being left without an ecclesiology, but hackneyed comments will not get to grips with this problem. We have to clarify and to structure the specific modality and original profiles through which Jesus is believed and the Church constructed in Latin America.

Faced with the Christian experience of the people, the theology of liberation is urged not only to take up again those subjects which signify the living of the faith by the people (popular theology) but to exercise a critical, purifying action especially in those sectors where the religious experience is in practice an alienating factor. The Christian majorities of Latin America are not living in a pagan environment, but they are not in the adult age of theological faith. A complex gamut of situations defines the intermediate Christian age which is characteristic of them. To restore popular values, to gain entry to their own symbolic universe, and to discern and make room for their own language is to prevent the theology of liberation from being converted into an "elitist theology" and to maintain it as a popular theology.

Finally, Gutiérrez speaks of "the novelty and mobility of the questioning" and of taking care not to fall "into intellectual self-satisfaction". Assmann speaks of "gaps in theology of long standing" and "exercises in option" and Dussel talks of carrying out the task in terms of "going for the historical, political, economic and cultural project of our peoples". Our conclusion must be that there are many theological themes which can only be truly elaborated by keeping in step with the effective advance of the process of liberation.

IV. A New Pastoral Style

Since Medellín, there has been talk of a "liberating pastoral activity". We can now affirm that, on the one hand, the content and understanding of liberation have grown clearer and more critical and, on the other, the concrete circumstances of its realization have altered abysmally. If in 1968 it was possible to speak almost euphorically of "liberation" and the stage was reached of thinking of a coalition of dispersed forces designed to get them moving towards the emancipation of the continent, the language, options, ways and forces have all now taken up radically opposed positions. Scientific analyses and political options have sharpened and polarized more and more people's viewpoints and postures. Five years after Medellín, liberation is no longer a subject for speculative polemics. It has begun to assume a very concrete expression in each situation, and this fact has faced the Church with the ineluctable challenge to take up a specific and effective attitude. The problem of the exact and palpable content of salvific statements is now widespread throughout all sectors of pastoral activity.

In the face of this problem the theology of liberation has made a clear option to evangelize from a position of solidarity with the exploited masses.

A pastoral action which really seeks out a response to specific demands and needs in all their complexity, and begins to proclaim the Christian Message from a position of real, effective solidarity with the interests and struggles of the poor, and of the exploited classes, is still a phenomenon only found abroad, outside Latin America.

Within the perspective of liberation, it is indisputably clear that this is the pastoral activity which makes it possible for the Church to be convoked by the liberating proclamation as an *ecclesia* of the poor, a Church of the people.[17]

How to understand and implement the efficacy of salvation in history, and how to be of true service to the historical process of liberation—this is the permanent challenge of a new style of pastoral activity. Now, with special urgency, the efficacy and significance of the presence of the Church in the world are measured by its aptitude and witness for the evangelization of the poor (Luke 4. 18). In the Latin American world of today, that means its capacity to make a decisive contribution to the liberation of man, and to the construction of a more just and fraternal society. For that reason the problem of the evangelization of the oppressed is closely linked to that of the prophetic character of Christians.

In the future, theological reflection about liberation will be much more intimately bound to those communities of believers who, rising from below, have committed themselves to liberty, and in the heart of the struggle hold fast to the certainty that to work for the passage to a new order of things according to faith, is to make the Church once more "a people with a paschal consciousness."

Translated by J. P. Donnelly

---

[17] *Ibid*. Cf. S. Galilea "¿A los pobres se les anuncia el evangelio?" *op. cit.*, p. 49.

Ronaldo Muñoz

Two Community Experiences in the Latin American Liberation Movement

I HAVE been asked to explain and analyse in this report some of the experiences of recent years which Christian groups and communities of Latin America have lived through in their involvement with the liberation movement. Because of shortage of space, I shall limit myself to two experiences, chosen from among the most typical—firstly, collective poverty as a situation of sin, and secondly, social liberation as an expression of faith. It should not be difficult to show, by using selected texts as my starting-point, the relationship in our life here between the mystical and the political dimensions of the Christian faith.

I. COLLECTIVE POVERTY AS A SITUATION OF SIN

The approach of the Church in Latin America to a new Christian praxis is not the result of a gratuitous search for a better understanding of the faith. Nor is it, primarily at least, the result of the impact of a new scientific view of the world and man. It is rather the result of an historical situation, and fundamentally of the fact of the poverty explosion. All the texts dealing with the new praxis recognize this. Let me quote as an example a particularly well-authorized text:

"Latin America appears to live still under the tragic sign of underdevelopment, which makes it impossible for our brothers not only to enjoy material goods, but also to fulfil themselves. Despite all the efforts that are made, we are faced with hunger and poverty, massive disease and infant mortality, illiteracy and

marginalism, profound inequalities of income and tensions between the social classes, outbreaks of violence and a scanty participation of the people in the management of the common good."[1]

The fact of poverty does not need theology to classify it as a
"sign of the times" to weigh on the Christian conscience; it
forces itself on us by its sheer weight and extent.

Especially since the Assembly of Medellín (1968), Christian
groups have gone further than a simple recognition of poverty—
they have also analysed its structural causes and worked out a
strategy of action. For this, they have had recourse to the techniques of the social sciences. The perception of poverty, however,
is a matter of experience or direct contact and its reality is proclaimed in a language which has more in common with that of
the prophets of Israel than with scientific analysis. Let me give
some examples of this language.

"We denounce the violence provoked by the rich and powerful,
because all usurpation of rights is a kind of violence."[2]

"We ask for a denunciation of ... the state of violence into
which those in power—individuals, groups and nations—have
plunged the peoples of our continent for whole centuries."[3]

"A new economic and political situation is to be fashioned
on the unemployment, hunger, misfortune, despair and death of
the workers."[4]

"In present circumstances, with the brutal pressures of the
structures of the system, in which hunger, poverty and idleness

[1] *The Church in the Present-Day Transformation of Latin America;
Documents of the Second General Assembly of Latin American Bishops*
(Bogotá, 1970); referred, in these footnotes, as *Medellín*.

[2] "200 Cristianos de Santiago, Manifiesto de la Iglesia joven (Santiago
de Chile, 1968)" in J. J. Rossi (Ed.), *Iglesia Latinoamericana ¿Protesta o
Profecía?* (Avellaneda, Argentina 1969), p. 214. Hereafter referred to as
Iglesia Lat.

[3] "900 Sacerdotes latinoamericanos, América Latina continente de vio-
lencia," in *Comisión Episcopal de Acción Social* (Ed.), *Signos de renovación*
(Lima, 1969), p. 106. Hereafter referred to as *Signos*. This document is
found in *Between Honesty and Hope: Documents from and about the
Church in Latin America, Issued at Lima by the Peruvian Bishops' Com-
mission for Social Action* (Maryknoll, New York, 1970), pp. 81–4.

[4] "Obispo y clero de San Andrés, Carta al Presidente del Brasil," in
Iglesia Lat, p. 171.

are the people's daily bread ... how can generous young people do anything but try to change this unjust state of affairs?"[5]

"It is essential to get to know the violence inflicted by the inhuman capitalist system ... on millions of human beings who live in oppression and helplessness."[6]

The word "violent" is used to describe the situation which keeps the Latin-American nations on the margin of common responsibilities and goods. Our capitalist society, with its subordination of human rights to economic results, is judged to be basically "violent". This description is justified in certain texts, for example: "... what is present here is not the inevitable consequence of a technically insoluble problem, but the unjust result of a situation which is deliberately maintained."[7]

These Christians, quite naturally and without making great distinctions, go from the ethical plane on which injustice and violence are diagnosed, to the religious plane:

"Does not the reality of our people shout out for more prophetic attitudes from priests and bishops? We believe so. We consider it a right and a duty to denounce as evil and sinful injustice in wages, the lack of bread, the exploitation of the poor and of the nation, the oppression of freedom."[8]

"The want of solidarity leads to real sin on the individual and the social plane, and this is crystallized in the unjust structures which mark the Latin-American situation."[9]

"We denounce and reject as contrary to the gospel any social organization which takes man as just another cog in the machine, and enslaves him in any way. In these situations we discover collective sin for which we are all, consciously or unconsciously, responsible."[10]

"This analysis makes it clear that our situation is unjust. This

[5] "Universitarios Cristianos de Sucre," *Comunicado sobre los compañeros que parten a la guerrilla* (Polycopied text).

[6] "Círculo 'Tercer Mundo' de Panamá, Carta abierta al Papa Pablo VIo (1968)" in *Iglesia Lat.,* p. 278.

[7] "900 Sacerdotes Latinoamericanos," *ibid.,* p. 104.

[8] "300 Sacerdotes brasileños, Declaración sobre la Iglesia y la realidad del Brasil (1967)" in *Signos,* p. 156.

[9] *Medellín,* Justicia, n. 2.

[10] "Encuentro Socio-Pastoral de Montevideo, Conclusiones," in: *Iglesia Lat.,* p. 391.

is an objective state of sin. The attitudes and decisions which create this situation are inhuman and therefore contrary to the gospel."[11]

"The present social structures, oppressive and dehumanizing, point to a situation of collective sin."[12]

The injustice and violence institutionalized in society, with their harvest of poverty and oppression for the majorities, are recognized as a sinful situation, a scandal "calling out to heaven", a provocation of God, who does not want poverty and hates injustice:

"In our country, the social, economic and cultural differences imply a social order which is unjust and is consequently opposed to the will of God."[13]

"In Latin America ... we must overcome situations which call out to heaven."[14]

"There are many studies of the human condition in Latin America. All of them describe the poverty which relegates large human groups to the margin. That poverty, as a collective fact, is an injustice calling out to heaven."[15]

"Where social, political, economic and cultural inequality and injustice are found, there also is a rejection of the Lord's gift of peace. Still more, there is a rejection of the Lord himself."[16]

"We are a group which wants to be a Church, which is angry in the face of oppression and injustice.... We can no longer remain unmoved faced with a situation which, according to Paul VI, 'calls out to heaven'."[17]

Here we must consider a fundamental question for any Christian reflection which aims to start from reality. Does this leap

[11] "14 Sacerdotes de San Juan, Manifiesto (1969)" in: *Iglesia Lat.*, p. 141.
[12] "20 Encuentro Nacional de ONIS, *Conclusiones* (Lima, 1969 polycopied) p. 29, English version in IDOCINA No. 4 (May 23, 1970), pp. 37-41.
[13] "Sínodo de Santiago," *Iglesia de Santiago, ¿qué dices de ti misma?* (Santiago de Chile, 1968), p. 106.
[14] "Equipos continentales de la Confederación Sindical Cristiana, Carta abierta de trabajadores latinoamericanos al Papa Pablo VIo" (Caracas, 1968) in: *Iglesia Lat.*, p. 85.
[15] *Medellín*, Justicia, no. 1.
[16] *Medellín*, Paz, no. 14.
[17] Universitarios Cristianos de México, Carta a los Obispos (Mexico, 1969 polycopied).

from the socio-economic to the religious plane correspond to a mere juridical approximation of two extrinsic orders? Or can it be justified by an interior relationship which is visible at least to faith? More specifically, when Latin American Christians begin to talk of "sin" in this context, are they simply applying a dogmatic solution to a social analysis? Or are they speaking of an experience which precedes such an analysis, discerns in the unjust oppression of the poor a more profound dimension, thrown into relief against the background of the absolute?

The second answer seems to be correct. "Sin" is referred to, not as a breach of a moral code received in the past from a distant, arbitrary God, but as an involvement of the living God in the injustice of this collective poverty. God himself is seen to be provoked by the violence of our society against the poor, and he provokes us to radical conversion and to act in consequence. In other words, behind this diagnosis of sin we can recognize that there is the assumption of an interior relationship or unity between social and religious reality. Within our consciousness of the injustice which oppresses the majorities, this unity can bring about a certain negative experience of God. The experience of social injustice therefore opens the way to our perception of the God of justice, the God who fixes the absolute value of man, caught up and trampled upon in the unjust situation.

We cannot interpret this way of experience simply as a kind of "propaedeutic" to faith in God. Faith certainly is seen here in the act of discovering and actualizing itself, but it is a faith which is present beforehand as enshrining that experience and as the framework within which that experience is articulated. In the case of Christian communities which reflect as such on social reality, we can recognize in their approach the *a priori* categories of a certain Christian vision of man and society. Within these categories, they perceive the inhumanity of the poverty which the majorities suffer and the injustice which operates in the established social order.

But something more is implied in speaking of a situation of sin—not only a Christian concept of man and society, but also a Christian concept of God. God is seen not only as giving commandments of justice from heaven for the faithful, but also as involved in the concrete history of society, identified with man and especially with the oppressed. By that very fact he is personally provoked by the suffering and oppression of the masses of the poor.

It follows that in our practical attitude when faced with the situation of injustice—an attitude of involvement or indifference —our own relationship with God is at stake, that is to say, the meaning or the futility of our whole lives. The justice that God requires of us is not seen as a juridical requisite against the revenge of his judgment in the life beyond, but as the all-consuming demand of his justice wounded here in the suffering of the oppressed, obliging us to act now in accordance with his liberating judgment in history. Because God himself—the living God of the patriarchs and prophets of Israel, the God of Jesus Christ and his witnesses of today—is found not so much in the pure recollection of solitary prayer as in the concrete history of our society, in our brothers and particularly in the most underprivileged and oppressed.

II. SOCIAL LIBERATION AS THE EXPRESSION OF FAITH

The most striking aspect of the Christian language of these Latin American communities is the way in which the gospel is referred to as a call to social justice, a message of liberation for peoples oppressed by poverty and exploited by an unjust social system. Examples of this are:

"The whole climate of the gospel is a continuous vindication of the right of the poor to make their voices heard, to be considered by society, to subordinate economic motives to the needs of the weakest. Was not Christ's first sermon preached to proclaim the liberation of the oppressed?"[18]

"Christ did not preach an individualistic religion. Turning its back on the temporal order, he said that justice and charity were the foundation of his Kingdom."[19]

"Why is the pope coming to Colombia? To bless poverty, to preach patience in injustice, to bless inhuman capitalism? Or is

[18] "21 Sacerdotes de Buenos Aires, Manifiesto (1967)" in: *Iglesia Lat.*, p. 106.
[19] "Obispo y 51 Sacerdotes de Costa Rica, Orden temporal y Redención (1968)" in: *Iglesia Lat.*, p. 238.

he coming like another Christ to denounce injustice in all its shapes, to commit himself to the suffering poor, to shout out to the rich the truth of the gospel?"[20]

"We cannot remain unmoved in the face of the injustice which afflicts the humblest people. Every Christian must apply evangelical values."[21]

"The Church's first duty is to preach the gospel to the poor. It has to liberate, humanize and develop the possibilities of the New Man."[22]

"Our aim must be to liberate man from every form of slavery —the lack of basic resources, illiteracy, the weight of social structures which deprive him of his responsibility, the materialistic concept of existence."[23]

"Today in Latin America ... the oppressed have wakened up to their needs and sufferings and their conditions must be improved. ... The Church respects all that we do to help them ... provided it meets the appeal for liberation of the oppressed, the poor and the afflicted which Christ himself left alive among us in his own person."[24]

Such statements are often taken as simple social proclamations or revolutionary slogans and their Christian jargon awakens the suspicion that the gospel is being used as an instrument of politics. The fact is that these formulae rarely appear with any theological explanation, and their religious context is not always clearly visible. The liberation that they proclaim seems to be directed exclusively towards the poor in the obvious sense of the word and the slavery from which they are to be liberated simply appears to be the poverty which is their lot in society.

If this were really the case, it would not be enough to excuse these Latin American Christians because of the world of poverty and injustice in which they live. Nor would it do to justify their

[20] "Cristianos de la Parroquia de Barrancas (Santiago de Chile), ¿Folklore o Cristianismo en Colombia? (1968)" in: *Iglesia Lat.*, p. 212.

[21] "Centro 'Juan XXIII' (San Juan), Adhesión al manifiesto de los sacerdotes de San Juan (1969)" in: *Iglesia Lat.*, p. 143.

[22] "Assamblea Pastoral de la Diocesis de Salto (Uruguay), Conclusiones (1968)" in: *Iglesia Lat.*, p. 377.

[23] "Los Jesuitas de Santo Domingo, Declaración ante la expulsión de dos sacerdotes extranjeros (1969)" in: *Iglesia Lat.*, p. 364.

[24] "Los Asesores universitarios de Sucre," *Nota al Comunicado de los*

position by a superficial reference to God's love of the poor in Scripture. A reference of this sort could well make for an ideological superstructure as illusory as the notion of God as the protector of the established order.

Formulae of this kind are of course, in a sense, slogans. They appear in short, ephemeral documents as a rapid confession of faith by groups who have no time for theological reflection. For that very reason, they have the strength and weakness of all slogans. Their strength is that they are clear-cut and concise, express the convictions of a group and give driving force to its common action. These groups are keenly aware of their commitment to social situations which demand swift, concerted and sustained action. But, like all slogans, they are liable to wear thin through constant use, cease to evoke their convictions in sufficient depth and reduce them to the concrete praxis. I do not deny that this danger is present on the path now being followed by these groups in the Latin American Church. But encouraged by experience and relying on the analysis of an important number of documents,[25] from which the texts just quoted were taken, I think it would be unjust to accuse these Christian groups of such a reduction of the gospel. In the broad context of these documents and frequently in the immediate context of the "slogans" which we are analysing here, we find, not a reduction of the gospel to social and political reform, but, on the contrary, a prophetic experience of our responsibilities in present history, in the light of the gospel of the Kingdom of God.

As regards the broad context, let me just list a few elements, several of which we have already met in the first part of this report: the diagnosis of "sin" with which the analyses of the situation are generally concluded; the religious basis of human dignity which can be seen to be trampled on among the poor; the recognition of the saving action of God in the everyday texture of human and social life, within which he calls for conversion and commitment; the recapitulation of the liberating action and questioning word of God in Jesus Christ, who shows

---

dirigentes estudiantiles (Sucre, 1970, polycopied).

[25] Cf. R. Muñoz, *Nueva Conciencia de la Iglesia en América Latina* (Santiago de Chile, 1973).

[26] Cf. Paul VI, *Populorum Progressio,* nos. 20-1.

us the transcendent dimension of all that is humanly valid and
the eschatological direction of history. As regards the immediate
context, a reading of some texts from the above documents and
from other, similar ones will reveal greater theological
elaboration:

"Just as in the past the Israelites experienced the salvific presence of God when he liberated them from the oppression of
Egypt and led them towards the promised land, so also we cannot
but feel his saving approach when we experience true development, which is the passage, for each and all of us, from a less
human state of life to a more human state."[26]

"In this transformation, behind which is expressed the desire
to integrate the whole scale of temporal values in the global
vision of the Christian faith, we become aware of the 'original
vocation' of Latin America."[27]

"In the history of salvation, the divine work is an action of
integral liberation and promotion of man in his whole dimension.... Love, the supreme commandment of the Lord, is the
dynamic power which must move Christians to bring about
justice in the world."[28]

"In the Kingdom of God which Jesus preached, the weakest
and the poor are the chosen, but no one is excluded from the
call of the Lord. Our solidarity with those who have fewer op-
portunities is a sign of the proclamation of the Good News of
liberation."[29]

"Jesus announces the arrival of the Kingdom of God ... in
favour of the poor and oppressed ... in a word, of the underprivileged and marginal in our society.... The Kingdom he
proclaims is essentially religious ... but communion with the
living God involves the transformation of the whole man: spirit
and body, person and community, and even the cosmos...."[30]

If our country engages in a great battle against poverty,
Christians, who must be fully committed to it, will feel that
whatever is achieved is a first realization of the Kingdom pro-

---

[27] *Medellín* "Introduction", n. 6–7.
[28] *Medellín* "Justica," n. 4.
[29] "Encuentro Socio-Pastoral de Montevideo," *ibid*.
[30] 4a. Asamblea de la Confederación Latinoamericana de Religiosos,
Pobreza y Vida Religiosa en America Latina (Bogotá, 1970), pp. 44–5.

claimed by Jesus.... Today the gospel of Jesus is proclaimed through the efforts of many men to achieve justice."[31]

We can group texts like these round three themes: (1) the biblical basis for the "slogan" of the liberation of the oppressed, (2) the gospel as a message not only of justice, but also of love and (3) the liberation of Christ as the integral liberation of man.

1. From the Old Testament, the most frequent reference is that which recalls the situation of the people of Israel captive and exploited in Egypt and the action of God who intervenes with Moses to liberate them. Various elements suggest a parallel between the situation of the Israelites and the present situation of the Latin American peoples. But rather than establish more or less facile "parallels", a more fertile approach in my view is the idea that God, whom we recognize today in our people's drive to free themselves from servitude, is the same God who revealed himself in the past to Moses as a liberator in history. At the same time we must not lose sight of the mediation of history itself.

But the biblical story is called especially to mind because of the central figure of Jesus Christ. It is always recalled that Christ took upon himself all mankind in all its wretchedness, and delivered himself up even to death. Along this path, he not only liberated mankind from eternal death, but through his resurrection he opened up the way to eternal fulfilment for all human liberations. It is remembered[32] that Jesus was above all the Messiah of the poor and Liberator of the oppressed. In Christ, then, we see the new, genuine Moses, who comes from God to free men of all their slavery, because at the root of slavery is sin.

2. Our Christian groups, though referring more frequently to justice, speak also of love as a characteristic demand of the gospel. The word "also" will doubtless surprise readers of the New Testament, who will be accustomed to the absolute primacy of love. I think that this relegation can be partly explained as a reaction against an ideological abuse in the preaching of love. For so long, good works have been advocated as a balm for the wounds of poverty. The structural conflicts of society

[31] "Los sacerdotes de la Parroquia Universitaria de Santiago, El presente de Chile y el Evangelio", in: *Mensaje* 196 (Feb. 1971), p. 37.
[32] With special reference to the witness of St Luke.

have been papered over with a false reconciliation. Even if this reaction is discounted, it seems normal enough that in a situation of injustice like that prevailing in Latin America, love— if it is to be as realistic and efficacious as the New Testament itself demands—should be expressed primarily as a demand for justice in favour of the oppressed, who form the majority of our brothers.

3. Finally, the texts which we are analysing affirm in various ways that the liberation they are speaking of is not only "spiritual" and religious, but human and integral.

Conscious of the newness of the Spirit, these Christians know that the nucleus of the Kingdom which Jesus inaugurates is religious: God himself in the person of the Son opens to men communion with his own life. But in the hope of the Old Testament, they also know that this community with the living God implies the transformation of the whole man, spirit and body, individual and society. The whole of creation will have to be freed for the service of man and re-created in Christ. If they insist, then, that the poor are the first in the Kingdom, it is because they are the ones who have most need of this integral liberation: "Blessed are those who hunger, for they shall be satisfied."

This is not the place to give a more critical analysis of these affirmations from the theological point of view. What is above all important is to show that, for the experience of these Latin American communities, the following elements are indissolubly united in an active faith in Christ the Liberator: the eradication of poverty and the possibility of spiritual growth—justice for the oppressed and love of all men; the concerted liberating effort of men and the recognition of God's liberating actions; the achievement in history of justice and brotherhood among men, and the advance towards the fullness of the Kingdom of God.

Translated by J. P. Donnelly

José Míguez Bonino

Popular Piety in Latin America

I

THE range and variety of the phenomena included under the heading of popular piety and the conflicting interpretations given to them make this a difficult subject to approach. However, its importance both in theory and practice means that it cannot be neglected if Latin American socio-political or religious questions are to be properly considered.

Popular forms of religion, as everyone knows, flourish all over Latin America in the shape of popular Catholicism, syncretic cults and sects and Protestant Pentecostalism. In a secularized modern city like Buenos Aires, the Feast of San Cayetano still draws a million devotees each year (one in every seven or eight inhabitants). In half a century, the Pentecostal movement has reached ten to twelve per cent of the population of Chile and it continues to grow rapidly in half a dozen Latin American countries. The Afro-American spiritualist cults have spread widely in the Caribbean and in Brazil, where it has reached even the middle classes.

There are, moreover, other important factors. The world-wide process of secularization takes on a different character in this region and is political rather than technological. The interaction between this process and popular piety has its own characteristics and these cannot be analysed and interpreted in the same way as those in North America.

We have already mentioned the complexity of the phenomenon. To begin with, it is not homogeneous. If we accept, with due reservations, a tripartite division of the regions of Latin

America, we will find a popular religiosity in the predominantly native regions (Mexico and the Pacific Coast), another in the regions influenced by African immigration (the Caribbean and Brazil), and another in those influenced by European immigration (the River Plate and part of Chile). The generalizations which we will make about this subject do not always apply in equal measure or in the same way to different forms of popular religiosity. To treat the subject in depth would demand a detailed consideration of these forms. In addition, the Protestant forms of popular piety—this is basically Pentecostalism—have their own characteristics to which we will briefly refer. These are accounted for by their historical matrix or by the sociological conditions in which they are produced.

The range of interpretations of popular religiosity is no less diverse. There are three ways of looking at it. These are not necessarily mutually exclusive but they are to some extent contradictory. The first interpretation, which is psycho-sociological, was initiated by the Belgian sociologist of religion, Emile Pin, and adopted with modifications by Aldo Büntig[1] in his extensive study of popular Catholicism in the Argentine. Büntig begins with an investigation of the *motives* for popular religiosity. He shows how the primary motives (cosmological, psychological, eschatological and individual) and to a lesser extent the secondary motives (integration into the group one belongs to) predominate over the socio-religious motives of spiritual transformation. This interpretation has been criticized for presupposing a schema of progress which discards primitive religiosity first and advances through a process of purification and spiritualization of motives towards secularization and individual autonomy.

The second interpretation studies popular piety within the framework of the "culture of poverty". Sociologists like Oscar Lewis have described and made a careful study of this culture in our continent. It is the phenomenon brought about by the

---

[1] See the work edited by A. Büntig, *El Catolicismo popular en la Argentina* (Buenos Aires, 1969). It is in five volumes. The first is sociological and was written by Büntig himself. A summary of the thesis and conclusions of the author are found in his article, "Dimensiones del catolicismo popular latinoamericano y su inserción en el proceso de liberación" in the composite book, *Fé cristiana y cambio social en América Latina* (Salamanca, 1973), pp. 129–50.

massive emigration of rural populations into the cities, a characteristic of the majority of Latin-American countries. (The proportions of rural and urban population, 70% and 30% respectively at the beginning of the century, will be reversed by the end of the twentieth century.) The individual is lost in the mass and beset by poverty and by psychic and family imbalance (anomia). He seizes hold of any form of security. His refuge is religiosity in the shape of ancient rites and mediators or in the form of new popular devotions or Pentecostalism.[2]

Finally, there have been attempts, especially by Enrique Dussel, to interpret Latin American popular religiosity within the framework of colonial Christianity in the light of the dominance and dependence present throughout the history of the continent.[3] We will return to this subject very shortly as it represents an important point of contact with the theme under consideration.

Although it is impossible to discuss these various hypotheses and interpretations in depth, it is important to keep them in mind when approaching the central theme of this article, which is the role of popular piety in the struggle for liberation in Latin America and particularly the political struggle.

II

Marx's well-known description of religion as a protest by and (false) consolation for the "enslaved creature" affords a useful point of reference for an examination of the significance of popular piety in the move towards political liberation in Latin America.

As Dussel has indicated, Latin America was set up as a colonial Christendom, a comprehensive system (religious, political, economic and social) whose juridical form was set in the *recopilación de leyes de Indias*, in other words, Spain's legal code for her

[2] For example, in the article of Mónica González Larraín (of the Instituto de Pastoral Latinoamericano of CELAM, generally known as IPLA) entitled "Catolicismo popular" in *Actualidad Pastoral* (May, 1972, no. 52, pp. 81–5). For the Pentecostal phenomenon, the work of Christian L. D'Epinay, *El refugio de las masas* (Santiago de Chile, 1966), esp. chap. 2.

[3] From the numerous works of Dussel we would draw attention to vols. 4 and 5 of *El catolicismo popular en la Argentina* (cf. note 1) and to his *Hipótesis para una Historia de la Iglesia en América Latina* (Barcelona, 1967).

South American colonies). Furthermore, as the historian of the sixteenth-century missions in Mexico and Peru, P. Ricard, has shown, what was founded in Latin America was not a Latin American Church but a Spanish Church transplanted with its buildings, laws, liturgy, feasts and devotions into Latin American soil. The encounter between the European Christian faith and the autochthonous cultures and religions of Latin America was inevitable, despite the general policy of *tabula rasa*. This encounter determined the popular religiosity of later ages and had other decisive effects. It explains the separation of popular piety from the hierarchical, institutional Church and the presence of certain elements of protest against that Church. Popular religiosity is to some extent the protest of the natives and the *mestizos*, who have been subjected to a foreign culture, religion and morality, but who use the names and forms of the latter to reconstitute the elements of their own religious and cultural identity.

This is not simply a theory. J. Comblin has described the characteristics of popular messianism (in north-east Brazil especially) as an expression of protest against and distrust of institutional religion and authority, and evidence of the anticipation, through miracles, of the establishment of a new kingdom of salvation and justice. These movements have in some cases been militant, and even violent.[4] In his study of Chilean Pentecostalism the Swiss sociologist Lalive d'Espinay sees in the "social strike" of the Pentecostals a manifestation of their protest "against an implacable society", against the "evil world" which they have experienced as poverty, sickness, rejection and death.[5]

The protest, however, is absorbed by religiosity and toned down into a kind of substitutive satisfaction. In the process, alas, it loses all its power to transform the individual and society. This clearly happens in the case of Pentecostalism. The believer encounters a supportive and sharing community and a number of ethical norms which allow him to achieve some social and economic progress. He transfers his final hope to heaven and anticipates it spiritually on earth in the community of the

[4] See for example the material presented in "El Cristo de la fé y los Cristos de América Latina" in *Vispera* 9 (1969).

[5] *Op. cit.,* pp. 158 ff.

Church. He loses solidarity with the struggle of his class, is integrated into the existing social order and becomes a political dead weight.

Those who have investigated popular Catholicism have also emphasized the conformist, passive attitudes which it engenders. Studies undertaken from different viewpoints agree on this question. A research student of IPLA[6] says: "the religiosity of poverty hardly ever transforms life". The director of EPLA comments: "It is well known that a Catholicism of this kind reinforces a dualist view of reality and therefore a religious attitude which is alienated from the world". He adds: "this popular Catholicism reinforces the social system of Latin America, with all its injustices, contradictions and oppressions".[7] Büntig's[8] investigations come to a similar conclusion. Originally interested in the values of popular Catholicism, he is now more concerned with the values of the people themselves and has concluded: "in our opinion, the process has moved from society to the Church". Even Dussel, who sees popular Catholicism as a legitimate reflection and expression of Latin American man, has concluded that it is "a manifestation of certain ontological needs of man in an unauthentic state and that, in a process of liberation, "it cannot be allowed to grow", because it reflects "a consciousness which is still childish and immature" and which must be transcended.[9] It would be difficult to find a harsher or more realistic summing-up of this situation than the following paragraph from the *Semana Internacional de Catéquesis* (Medellín, 1968): "Manifestations of popular religiosity may at times contain positive elements, but they are, in the present rapid evolution of society, above all the expression of alienated groups. This, of course, means those groups whose way of life is despersonalized, conformist, uncritical and lacking any will to change society.

[6] Mónica González Larraín, *op. cit.*, p. 82.
[7] Segundo Galilea, "La fé como principio crítico de promoción de la religiosidad popular" in *Fé cristiana y cambio social en América Latina*, p. 152.
[8] See above (note 1).
[9] "Orientaciones y conclusiones de la Semana Internacional de Catequesis," Com. 6. No. 3, quoted by Leonor Ossa, *Die Revolution—das ist ein Buch und ein freier Mensch* (Hamburg, 1973), p. 35.

This kind of religiosity is maintained and in part stimulated by the dominant structures, to which the Church belongs, and above all it acts as a brake on any move to change the structures of society."

These critical considerations are reinforced when one considers the political use which is made of popular religiosity of this type to prevent the masses from protesting against or from transforming the establishment. It is therefore worth drawing attention to three points:

1. It is well known that ideological use can be made of an "order of creation" to justify the established structures of society. What is less widely known perhaps is the prevalence of this kind of ideology in rural and marginal areas in Latin America. Misery is theologically rationalized as "sin" (indolence, laziness or inferiority), as "bad luck" or, still worse, as the nature of things, in other words, the will of God. "It has always been that way and always will be" is the explanation given time and again to investigators and it is often added: "you've just got to put up with it."

2. More recently, the "campaigns of terror" unleashed by conservative political propaganda in Chile, Uruguay and other countries appeal to "Christian values" (the family, freedom and law and order) to warn the people against revolutionary movements and ideologies. The best organized and most virulent expressions of this reactionary political mobilization of religious consciousness are to be found mainly in the middle and upper sectors of Latin American society, such as the movements of *Tradición, Patria y Propiedad*, and in terrorist groups of right-wing Catholic sectors. We cannot, however, ignore the weight which this appeal to the defence of "Christian ways of life" still has in populations which consider themselves Catholic.[10]

3. Finally, the ideology of peace at any price is always based on the Christian commandment of love, which is opposed to any mobilization of the people in favour of a transformation of the political and economic structures of society. It is worth noting

[10] On this point see the article of Hugo Assmann, "El cristianismo, su plusvalía ideologica y el costo social de la revolución socialista," in H. Assmann, *Teología desde la praxis de la liberación* (Salamanca, 1973), pp. 171–97.

that even the ecclesiastical documents in which the conditions of injustice of Latin American society are denounced, and in some cases in which their structural causes made plain, generally conclude on the same note. The oppressors are exhorted to change the situation and a warning is given (either explicitly or implicitly aimed at the oppressed people) against all forms of violence. Whatever one's judgment about the various forms that struggle can take, it is difficult to deny the paralysing nature of many of these exhortations. Rather than giving an impetus to solidarity in the struggle for transformation, Christian love becomes an obstacle in the continuation of that struggle.

III

Neither on the basis of history nor on that of the current state-of affairs can popular piety, in its Catholic, Protestant or other forms, be absorbed from the harsh charges brought against it by the members of the *"Semana de Catéquesis"*. This is not the end of the story, however, and for two reasons. The first is theoretical—popular religiosity cannot lightly be put aside, if it is hoped to integrate the masses of the Latin American people in the work of their own liberation. The second reason is that, in Latin America, more and more attempts are being made to direct popular religiosity towards the task of political and social transformation. Only a few general observations can be made here about this potential of popular religiosity to transform society.
1. We pointed out at the beginning of this article that secularization in Latin America was leading to greater political awareness rather than to technological evolution. The former creates a revolutionary ethos which embraces the whole of life and activity, while the latter functionalizes every sphere of human life. This ethos reflects a vision of the world and of history and is reflected in symbols and actions which both express it and appeal to men to commit themselves. The relationship between these manifestations and those found in religion is immediately apparent. No further proof of this will be needed for anyone who is familiar with the christological setting given to Che Guevara or Camilo Torres in revolutionary iconography or ballads, or with the popular rituals of certain political manifestations or

social protests. A revolutionary process both calls for and stimulates an atmosphere of enthusiasm with religious overtones.

2. This fact has led some Christians, who are committed to the struggle for the social and political liberation of the people, to ask themselves if popular religiosity cannot be mobilized in favour of the struggle. The aim is not, however, an instrumentalization of popular religiosity. When Büntig speaks of "filling with the Word" the actions of popular Catholicism or when Galilea speaks of "evangelizing popular Catholicism", they propose to liberate this popular religiosity and transform it. Two complementary leads are given by these statements. One springs from the discovery, strongly emphasized by Büntig, that attitudes of openness, solidarity, and availability to one's neighbour's needs exist in the oppressed people and are the matrix of a revolutionary consciousness. The other starts from the rediscovery of the liberating context of the prophetic message of the Old and New Testaments.

3. This is not a case of simple theoretical possibilities. The concrete task of awakening a new consciousness which many priests and religious (and especially nuns) are carrying out in rural areas and of transforming what takes place at some traditional popular shrines (a good example is that of San Cayetano in Buenos Aires, which has already been referred to) are already showing concrete, positive results which have even attracted the attention of non-Christian observers. A good counter-proof of their importance is the alarm shown in conservative circles and the virulence of attacks conducted against these movements. These efforts cannot be described here, but it is important to point out that they exist.

4. There is no denying the fact, however, that the application of this transforming potential of the faith has also caused a crisis in popular religiosity. Perhaps it would be more correct to say that the real transforming potential of faith is only revealed when it leads to a crisis in popular religiosity. Many of the actions, devotions and symbols of popular religiosity furnish a "magic" substitute for human initiative and action. When the structural relationship between capitalism and unemployment or the social causes of infant mortality are discovered, the believer's attitude towards the saint from whom he sought work or

the health of his family changes. A new faith, rather than a mere growth in faith, comes about. However this change is brought about, this alienating popular piety must die, so that a responsible, adult faith may be born. Among Latin American theologians, Juan Luís Segundo has given the most trenchant account of this problem. The qualitative change involved in the passage to a mobilizing faith implies a corresponding re-evaluation of the role of the Church and of theological and pastoral tasks ahead. Conscious, committed Christian minority groups must necessarily be formed. In the end, this is the only form of community which suits the gospel commitment.[11]

5. To Segundo's radical solution, all the well-known objections about elitism are made, but these need not be gone into here. The opposition is based on what might be called "populism" and begins with the recognition that popular piety, even with all its alienations and contradictions, is a genuine manifestation of the culture of an oppressed people, reflecting a real protest against oppression and connected to the liberating values of the gospel. What is required of pastoral action is to de-alienate this piety and bring it to the maturity of a transforming, active and conscious faith. This pastoral approach is being tried in many places in Latin America. *Mutatis mutandis*, the same options are encountered in Protestantism in relation to pentecostal religiosity. What is happening here is the familiar pattern of divergence in policy between mass movements and advanced groups, between processes involving a progressive slow growth in consciousness and radical changes.

6. From the theological as well as the political angle, the popular piety which existed and still predominates in Latin America can only be regarded as profoundly alienated and alienating, a manifestation of a slave consciousness and an instrument for the continuation and consolidation of oppression. The attempt to transfer the dynamic power of this piety to the task of transforming without radically altering the content of religious consciousness itself, appears to be both psychologically and sociologically impossible as well as theologically unacceptable. Even if it can be achieved, it would only substitute one form of alie-

[11] J. L. Segundo, *Acción pastoral latinoamericana; sus motivos ocultos* (Buenos Aires, 1972) and *Masas y Minorías* (Buenos Aires, 1973).

nation for another. It would be the satanic temptation which
Jesus rejected, to substitute the miracle for the Word, and to give
bread without the adventure of faith looking for the Kingdom
of God. What is needed is the conversion and de-alienization of
this piety. This brings us up against a dialectical process. On the
one hand, consciousness is de-alienated only through a praxis
of liberation, to the extent that it accepts solidarity in the struggle for the transformation of the world. On the other, man's
consciousness has to be set free so that he can accept this praxis
and, in this sense, there is an initial pastoral action—if only
the symbolic presence of the priest or minister in the struggle
for liberation—which will (even through some of the mechan-
isms of the traditional piety) clear the way and give encourage-
ment. It is most important to recognize the limited, transitory
character of this action, and not to sacralize it in a new alienation
of the religious consciousness. In the last resort, there is no true
process of liberation without the creation in it and through it
of a new liberated consciousness, committed to solidarity. And
this points to the transcendence of an alienated, dehumanizing
religiosity, and the birth of a new consciousness of faith, a real
metanoia. Such a conversion cannot be brought about by religious
manipulations or "magic" liturgical transmutations, but only if
the Churches are ready to stand by the oppressed people in
solidarity with them, in the painful but joyful path of their
liberating struggle. From this position of solidarity the Churches
can encourage, console, give hope and spur to action. The Church
will then be a true sign of the liberating presence of the crucified
Lord, resurrected and coming among his people.

Translated by J. P. Donnelly

Biographical Notes

LEONARDO BOFF, O.F.M. was born in Concórdia in 1938, studied philosophy and theology in Curitiba, Petrópolis and Munique and was ordained in 1964. He gained his doctorate at the University of Munique and is now professor of systematic theology in the Institute of Philosophy and Theology at Petrópolis (Rio de Janeiro). He is also the editor of the *Revista Eclesiástica Brasileira*. His most important publications are *Die Kirche als Sakrament im Horizont der Welterfahrung* (Paderborn, 1972); *O Evangelho do Cristo cómico* (Petrópolis, 1970); *Jesus Cristo Liberatador* (Petrópolis, 1972), *Vida para além da morte* (Petrópolis, 1973) and *O destino do homem e do mundo* (Petrópolis, 1973).

JOSÉ MÍGUEZ BONINO was born in Santa Fé (Argentina) in 1924. He became a licentiate in theology at the Faculty of Protestant Theology of the University of Buenos Aires (1948), gained an M.A. in teaching at Emery University (U.S.A.) in 1953 and a TH.D. at the Union Theological Seminary of New York in 1960. He is a pastor of the Evangelical Methodist Church in Argentina and was ordained presbyter in 1948. He has served as a pastor in Cochabamba (Bolivia), San Rafael (Mendoza, Argentina) and Ramos Mejía (Buenos Aires, Argentina). From 1954 until 1970, he was a professor at the Faculty of Protestant Theology at Buenos Aires, specializing in systematic theology and comparative (Christian) religion. He was dean of the faculty from 1960 until 1969. At present he is a professor at the Higher Institute of Protestant Theological Studies and in charge of the department of postgraduate studies. He has been a delegate at the assemblies of the World Council of Churches and a member of various commissions of the Council. He was also an observer of the Methodist Church at the Second Vatican Council. His publications include *El nuevo mundo de Dios* (Buenos Aires, 1954); *Concilio abierto* (Buenos Aires, 1967); *Polémica, diálogo y misión* (Buenos Aires, 1967) (as editor); *Ama y haz lo que quieras* (Buenos Aires, 1972) and numerous articles, especially about the situation in Latin America and the Roman Catholic Church there, both in European and in American journals.

JOSEPH COMBLIN was born on 22 March 1923 in Brussels and was ordained priest in 1947. He is a doctor of theology and was expelled from Brazil in

1972 after having taught theology for seven years at Recife. He is now teaching at the Catholic University of Chile (Talca) and is also a professor at the Catholic University of Louvain. His publications include *Théologie de la Ville* (Paris, 1968) and *Théologie de la révolution* (Paris, 1970).

ENRIQUE DUSSEL was born in La Paz in 1934. He is a professor of history and philosophy at the Latin American Pastoral Institute (IPLA), which is a branch of CELAM at Quito (Ecuador). He is also professor of ethics at the University of Cuyo. He has published *Hipótesis para una historia de la Iglesia en América latina* (1967), the second edition of which will be found in *América latina en la Historia de la salvación* (1492-1971) (Barcelona, 1972); *El humanismo semita* (Buenos Aires, 1969); *Historia del catolicismo popular en Argentina* (Buenos Aires, 1970), *Para una destrucción de la historia de ética* (Paraná, 1972) and *La dialéctica hegeliana* (Mendoza, 1972).

SEGUNDO GALILEA was born in Santiago (Chile) in 1928 and was ordained priest in 1956. From 1963 onwards, he collaborated in the Pastoral Section of CELAM, the Episcopal Council of Latin America, first in Mexico, then in Ecuador. At present, he is the director of the Latin American Pastoral Institute (IPLA) which is part of CELAM. His publications include *Hacia una Pastoral Vernácula* (1964); *Para una Pastoral Latinoamericana* (1968); *Reflexiones sobre la Evangelización* (1969); *A los Pobres se anuncia el Evangelio?* (1971); *Contemplación y Apostolado* (1972); *Espiritualidad de la Liberación* (1973). He has also written many articles on pastoral questions in Latin America.

CLAUDE GEFFRÉ, O.P., was born in 1926 in Niort (France) and ordained priest in 1953. He studied at the Dominican Faculties of the Saulchoir. Doctor of theology (1957), he taught and was regent of studies at the Saulchoir. Since 1968, he has been professor of fundamental theology at the Faculty of Theology of the Institut Catholique in Paris. Among his published works are *Un espace pour Dieu* (Paris, 1970); *Un nouvel âge de la théologie* (Paris, 1972); in collaboration, *Procès de l'objectivité de Dieu* (1969); *Herméneutique et Eschatologie* (1971); *Révélation de Dieu et langage des hommes* (1972) and the articles on "God" and "Theology" in the *Encyclopaedia Universalis* (Paris).

GUSTAVO GUTIÉRREZ was born in Lima (Peru) in 1928. He is a licentiate in psychology (University of Louvain) and in theology (Lyons, France). He is the national adviser to UNEC, the National Union of Catholic Students in Peru and professor in the departments of theology and social sciences at the University of Lima. His publications include *La Pastoral de la Iglesia latinoamericana* (Montevideo, 1968) and *A Theology of Liberation* (Maryknoll, 1973).

RONALDO MUÑOZ was born in 1933 in Santiago (Chile). After having studied architecture, he entered the Congregation of the Sacred Heart (Picpus) in 1954. He studied philosophy and theology in Los Perales (Chile) and was later ordained priest (1961). He is a licentiate in theology (Gregorian

University, Rome, 1962) and a doctor qualified to teach at the Institut Catholique at Paris (1963). From 1964 onwards, he has divided his time between teaching (since 1966 at the Faculty of Theology of the Catholic University of Chile) and advising in theology in various communities and Church organizations in Chile and elsewhere in Latin America. He gained a doctorate in theology at the University of Regensburg (Germany) in 1972 after writing a thesis on the new consciousness of the Church in Latin America, which has since been published as *Nueva Conciencia de la Iglesia en América Latina* (Santiago, Chile, 1973).

JUAN SEGUNDO, S.J., was born on 31 October 1925 at Montevideo (Uruguay) and was ordained priest in 1955. He studied at the Faculty of Jesuit Theology at Louvain and at the Faculty of Literature at the University of Paris. He possesses a licentiate in theology and a doctorate in literature (1963). He was at one time director of the Centre at Montevideo for Social Study and Action, the Centro Pedro Fabro. His published works include *Berdiaeff. Une conception chrétiene de la Personne* (Paris, 1963) and *La Cristianidad, una utopía?* (Montevideo, 1963). He has also written *Theology for Artisans of a New Humanity* (five volumes, New York, 1973).

RAÚL VIDALES is a Mexican priest. He is a licentiate in theology and sociology and has studied in Mexico, the United States and Rome. At one time, he was professor of sociology at the University of Monterrey in Mexico. He has also taught at various universities in South America and, when he was a professor at the Latin American Pastoral Institute (IPLA), he gave lectures on political theology in Central and South America. Among other books, he has written *La Iglesia latinoamericana y la politica después de Medellín* and *El Espiritu que renueva*. He has also contributed to many journals specializing in theology and pastoral theology such as *Servir, Christus* and *Contact* in Mexico and *Actualidad Pastoral* in Argentina.